2017 edition

The Boston Economy

Understanding and Accessing One of
the World's Greatest Job Markets

D1451208

George Donnelly

Print edition first published in January, 2016

Second edition (2017 edition) published in January, 2017

Notices:

This book covers a constantly moving target, the Boston economy and many its businesspeople and companies, and some information may be out of date by the time this book reaches your hands.

Product or corporate names in this book may be trademarks or registered trademarks and are only used for informational purposed without intent to infringe.

ISBN: 978-0-9971132-2-8 (print edition)

Dedication

To Marcela for her unflagging support; and to Helen and Dan Donnelly.

Acknowledgements and special thanks

I couldn't have completed this book without a lot of help, particularly from a team of freelancers who contributed a handful of chapters and sections of other chapters. They include Jay Fitzgerald, Eric Convey and Sara Castellanos, whose knowledge of Boston's history and economy is vast and was extremely helpful for this project.

As a newbie in the self-publishing game, I learned as I went along. The designers for this book, Mark Gabrenya and Heather Hopp-Bruce, were critical in bringing it to life.

And a special thanks to Bill Brett for allowing me to use his wonderful photographs; and to all those who believed in the idea of this book and took the time to give advice or be interviewed.

Contents

The Boston economic advantage
— an introduction

No region in the country takes its economic success more for granted than Boston. It has an unmatched hospital ecosystem; the world's number one biotech cluster; and the largest and most potent assemblage of universities on Earth. And many of its other sectors are either at the top or near the top in the nation, including financial services, tech startups, and medical devices. The area's commercial real estate industry is on a tear. Foreign interest in Boston, in terms of tourism and investment, is at an all-time high.

To this whopping success, Bostonians almost seem to shrug their shoulders, especially about the prowess of their higher education system. Indeed, the region's built-in advantage is the 500,000-plus college students in Massachusetts who provide the raw material for economic growth. These students work hard through school, and often land internships to make connections with the "real world." But few of them understand the full scope of the opportunities around them. If you're one of those students, *The Boston Economy* is for you.

This book is designed to open your eyes to the talented people and innovative companies and institutions that are driving the Boston economy. Consider it both a primer on Boston business and a research tool.

We hope to put many companies on your personal radar screen that you otherwise wouldn't know about. For while there are many corporate giants here — over 40 publicly traded companies pull in over $1 billion in annual revenue — there also are thousands of small, private companies that are aggressively growing and hiring.

This book also puts Boston's various sectors in context. How did it become a leader in high-tech? What forces gathered to make it the world's biotech capital? The common thread for Boston's economic success is brainpower — the inspiration of smart people who saw opportunities and innovated in their respective fields. Boston's critical mass of talent has been the catalyst for groundbreaking advances that have led to many multi-billion dollar companies. And the deep well of human capital continues to pay huge dividends.

Too many students fend for themselves, and may not realize all that Boston has to offer. Talented graduates will find their own way, for sure, but how many of the best does the region lose because we didn't bother to make a simple pitch for them to start their careers here?

Key themes in *The Boston Economy*

The Greater Boston economy enjoys an embarrassment of riches. Perhaps no regional economy in the country has more depth and balance than Boston. Its strength in life sciences is matched by its success in high-tech and startup formation. It is a constantly changing economy and because of its many moving parts, difficult to catalog. This book attempts to capture a critical mass of it. Boston continues to sprout new companies that are emerging as leaders in cyber security, ecommerce, big data, robotics and digital marketing, just to name a few sectors.

The opportunities for emerging students to enter the Boston area economy are undersold. We don't do enough to harness Boston's one true natural resource: college graduates. Although there have been some new efforts to connect students with business through internship websites, the vast majority of students know little about the opportunities around them. While Boston's powerful economy is full of opportunity, to an emerging student or a young professional, it often seems like a confusing amalgamation with thousands of moving parts. Boston sometimes pays a price for its lack of self-promotion when our most in-demand students often are recruited away by the big names in Silicon Valley. How many more would stay if they knew more about opportunities in Boston? And how many more students would stay in the region, rather than return home to other states, if they had more exposure to local job opportunities?

Technology is rapidly transforming the economy, and thus, jobs. This may seem like a truism, but what may not be fully understood is how technology is affecting what we think of as the traditional economy. The new economy and what's referred to as the "old" economy are merging. There's increasingly little left of the non-tech economy – health care is on its way to becoming fully digitized, financial services is more technical than ever, and most manufacturers have fully embraced automation. On a practical level, this makes it harder for students to be "job ready" when they graduate, and places a greater premium on connecting with companies while they are undergraduates.

Boston is increasingly international. Boston has been discovered, and not only by European and Asian tourists. International students, global real estate investors, and companies and startups from all over the world are enhancing and reshaping the regional economy. And the internationalism goes both ways, with Boston companies increasingly expanding abroad. This creates great opportunities for students interested in global business.

All the same, the Boston economy faces significant challenges. The higher education business model is under stress. The traditional health care business model is undergoing transformation while facing more regulation, squeezing dollars out of the system. Financial services companies are migrating jobs out of state to more affordable locations. Housing costs are growing. The gap between those who have reaped the rewards from the Boston economy and those who haven't continues to grow.

The Boston Economy: Understanding and Accessing One of the World's Greatest Job Markets is designed to be a roadmap for those looking to navigate the local economy. And while it's impossible to capture every aspect of the regional economy, we see it as a perpetual work in progress, a book that will be updated regularly with new people, companies and insights.

Growing sectors and the hottest jobs and companies in Boston

The Boston economy has rebounded sharply from the so-called "Great Recession" of 2008-2009. It took a while for hiring to take hold: In January 2010, Massachusetts had an unemployment rate of 8.8 percent, a historically very high number that only looked good relative to the national rate, which was 9.8 percent. About 3.16 million Massachusetts residents were employed then. Fast forward five years, and almost 300,000 more people hold jobs in the state. In August 2015, the unemployment rate in Massachusetts was 4.7 percent.

When we break down those jobs by category, we get a better sense of where the hottest growth areas have been:

	Sept. 2016	Sept. 2010	% change
Professional and business services	552,400	463,900	19.1
Education and health services	793,200	689,100	15.1
Construction	149,700	107,000	39.9
Financial activities	223,800	214,200	4.5
Manufacturing	251,000	253,600	-1.0

The state's broad category of professional/business services has expanded considerably, as has the field of education, fueled by the hundreds of colleges in the state. Construction, which was anemic in 2009, is booming in the Boston area, as the demand for more space from the most innovative industries — like drug development — has been increasing for years. But one important sectors, manufacturing, continues to decline as companies opt for cheaper areas to build factories. Massachusetts manufacturers tend to produce sophisticated, high-value goods, like medical devices and semiconductors. Even as the number of manufacturing jobs has flattened, manufacturers often struggle to find an adequate supply of skilled workers.

Among the hottest job categories:

Biotech: Massachusetts may be one of the best places in the world to find a job for those who study biology or chemistry. Burning Glass predicts that Bay State biotechs will add 4,325 jobs in the three years ending in May 2018, a 6.7 percent increase. In a recent survey, 87 percent of the more than 20 major local biotech employers said they expect to add jobs in the next year.

Accounting: The return of a strong stock market and the many IPOs of tech and biotech startups has been good news for the local accounting industry. The state's Labor and Workforce Development Office projects a 12 percent increase in accounting jobs by the year 2022.

Information technology and big data: Massachusetts leads the nation in the concentration of its workers in the tech industry, and despite its relatively small size, it comes in fifth in sheep number of employees working in the tech sector, according to the Cyberstates 2016 report by CompTIA.

What are the hottest jobs?

Tracy Burns, CEO of the Northeast Human Resources Association, expects the biggest growth in coming years to continue to be in the field of STEM jobs — those focused on science, technology, engineering and math. She sees engineering jobs of all kinds — particularly civil, chemical and biotech — in high demand, while software engineers are always in short supply in Massachusetts. Aside from engineering but also likely to be grow quickly are positions for actuarialists.

"I think people are getting more practical about their education," Burns said. Many grads are leaning toward majors with widely applicable skills as opposed to ones centered on the liberal arts.

However, she says, liberal arts majors shouldn't despair.

"There are still companies out there willing to take liberal arts majors that have passion and are coachable," she said. Wayfair, for example, routinely hires entry-level positions for its call center, and she's seen fast advancement for motivated employees. "It's a good way to get into retail," she said. Also, lots of jobs in health care, higher education and financial services don't rely on math or science expertise.

Regardless, she strongly endorses students to seek out internships or other opportunities to work in a company before hitting the job market.

"I do think there's some expectation that these kids come out with some experiences," he said.

Fred Goff, CEO of the Boston-based career social networking site Jobcase, said he's seen increases in activity around health care, sales and administrative jobs in the past couple of years among the four-year college graduates on his site. Meanwhile, searches of his site for legal jobs have dropped.

But like Burns, he sees one overarching trend: A preference for employees who have an ability to deal with data. Even if a potential job-seeker doesn't plan to specialize in data science, he or she should be comfortable and familiar with it, he said.

"If you have the capability of speaking data — whatever job you're in — that's going to be the differentiation of value," he said. "The liberal arts majors that are proficient enough to understand the conversation of data... if they can translate that inside and outside, I think that we're finding a really necessary layer."

He said that the terms for that layer of employees who translate between data and what he calls the "softer skills" vary between companies: Some call it "customer success," while at others it's called "account management."

Goff also sees a trend toward not only switching companies, but changing entire careers more often than in the past

"Most skills are transferrable across industries, which means that these domain spaces have really broken down and we've now defined things more by your skill proficiencies," he said.

In-demand skills

Below is a list of some of the hottest jobs and in-demand skill sets in the Boston market:

Information security analyst: This field is the fastest growing in technology and software, and Boston is considered one of the top areas in the country

— second only to Silicon Valley — in leading the way in cybersecurity.

Computer systems analyst : Analysts are not simply "number crunchers," but they design computer systems for clients. Degrees are desired in math and/or statistics, computer science MBA or a master's degree with focus on analytics.

Web developers: These are tech workers who make sure websites are working properly, and figure out how to maximize and measure traffic. Google AdWords certification is something most companies highly prefer or either require, according to HireMinds, along with Google Analytics, Google and Bing Campaign expertise.

Human resources manager: People who are able to manage a company's most important resource — its employees — are needed at all companies and are potentially lucrative. A bachelors or master degree is usually all that's needed, and the field is expected to grow at an above-average rate through at least 2020.

Communications specialist: The term "communications" spans traditional public relations roles (including media and analyst relations to driving social media strategies) to marketing communications positions where candidates are focused on marketing collateral, white papers, online content (blogs, social, etc.) and trade shows. Candidates with degrees in marketing or English/journalism, and have, of course, strong writing ability.

Social media specialist: Every organization, including smaller firms, needs experts in online branding and marketing to make sure the company is active enough on a daily basis in posting updates and monitoring social media sites. At the minimum candidates should be familiar with social platforms like YouTube, Twitter, Facebook, Pinterest, and social analytics tools like Sprout Social and Hootsuite.

> Every organization needs social media managers to make sure the company is active enough on a daily basis.

Statisticians: There is a high demand for people who can crunch data and present it in easily-accessible formats, pointing out trends and anomalies. As the explosion in the amount of big data continues, those who can make sense of it and differentiate what is statistically significant from what's not are going to continue to be in high demand.

Biological scientists: Fueled by the Boston-area's boom in biotechnology and drug development companies, and that field's ongoing shift toward biological rather than chemical methods of production, scientists who know the ins and outs of living cells and organisms are needed. Particularly as the region becomes known for biological drug manufacturing, it's a skill set that will be in demand for years to come.

The competition for engineering talent ramps up

The demand for software engineering talent in Boston has become intense, compelling companies to adopt new recruiting strategies. In an October 2015 story in the Boston Globe, tech columnist Scott Kirsner describes a variety of efforts to either hire away or develop software engineers. Some companies, including Wayfair, the home goods ecommerce company, are developing in-house training programs for those with the fundamental engineering and math skills.

13 of the Boston area's hottest companies

Many companies in Boston are looking for a lot of talent as they grow rapidly. Here are some of the largest and most aggressive in terms of adding jobs:

General Electric, which just moved its headquarters to Boston in 2016, is a multinational conglomerate involved in a number of different industries, but is increasingly betting its future on being a developer of software. Its new South Boston headquarters is slated to employ 800 people, but it also has a large presence in Marlborough for its life sciences business and will likely be expanding elsewhere.

Wayfair is an ecommerce site specializing in home good that did $2.25 billion in revenue in 2015 and employs around 5,600. Headquartered in Boston, it hires sales representatives constantly and is on a major growth trajectory as it focuses on expanding internationally.

Shire, which specializes in drugs for rare diseases, is headquarterd in Lexington but has locations in Cambridge. It is projected to be the fast-est-growing drug company in the world through 2022, quickly eclipsing some of the more longstanding Bay State drugmakers like Biogen and Sanofi Genzyme. The company had more than 3,000 Massachusetts-based employees as of the summer of 2016 and is aiming at $20 billion in revenue by 2020.

Ernst & Young, grew its number of CPAs by 33 percent as of early 2016 from the year prior, becoming one of the biggest local accounting firms.

Abiomed: which makes medical implant devices, is headquartered in Danvers, and has grown the 800 employees there as well as its office in Germany. It has had a string of successes with its Impella heart pump, leading to a 43 percent year-over-year revenue growth last year.

The demand for software engineering talent in Boston has become intense, compelling companies to adopt new recruiting strategies.

LogMeIn, a tech company that creates remote access tools for computers (and is a leader in creating Internet of Things products), plans to add about 400 jobs over several years as part of its ongoing expansion in South Boston. A multitude of sales and engineering jobs populate its career site, including several positions in Europe.

TripAdvisor is a fast-growing travel site that recently completed a new 282,000-square-foot headquarters on Route 128 in Needham, Mass., moving 1,000 employees there with room for 500 more. Its career site has an array of jobs in sales, marketing, engineering, and data analytics.

Intarcia Therapeutics, a Boston biotech is hoping for FDA approval for a new treatment for Type 2 diabetes in fall of 2017, and is hoping to double in size to around 500 employees in coming years. It's raised more than $1 billion from investors to date.

WordStream: Based in Boston, the company develops search marketing software and sells managed pay-per-click advertising services. It had more than 150 employees in 2015 and more than doubled its revenue in the previous year.

HubSpot: The Boston-based inbound sales and marketing platform surpassed 1,000 employees worldwide in 2015, and continues to grow at an impressive rate. It was on track for about $270 million in revenue for 2016, a five-fold increase over the previous year.

Liberty Mutual, the second largest property and casualty insurer in the U.S., has increased its in-state headcount by over 1,000 in recent years. And despite its construction of a new Texas facility for 5,000 employees, it will continue to add jobs in Massachusetts. Liberty Mutual has said it will hire 25,000 employees over the next five years.

Athenahealth has experienced rapid growth in the electronic medical records field and planned to add jobs at various facilities across the country, including its Watertown, Mass. headquarters.

Pixability: The Boston-based ad buying and video marketing platform for YouTube was one of the fastest-growing private companies by revenue in 2016, according to the Boston Business Journal. With operations in New York, San Francisco, Chicago and London, the company serves media buyers, ad agencies, and marketers.

Why Boston? The case for building a career here

It's the story that still haunts Boston: Mark Zuckerberg, a Harvard student, left Cambridge a decade ago to set up headquarters in Silicon Valley for his burgeoning social network platform, Facebook. Massachusetts tech leaders and politicians have remained disheartened ever since that the state didn't nurture what eventually became a $370 billion company.

Indeed, Boston doesn't win them all (although Facebook has returned to Cambridge with a small foothold and has about 100 employees, a small consolation prize). But Facebook is the aberration, the cautionary tale, and not the rule. For the many who choose to stay, Boston offers a unique combination of brainpower, international access and innovative spirit that can quickly propel a career. Opportunities abound for ambitious talent.

Of course, given the inflow from around the world to the region's many higher education institutions, the outflow also is considerable. That observation was the genesis of a recent study published by venture firm Flybridge Capital and recruitment marketing company NextWave Hire. "Because the flow of students and out of Massachusetts is such a strategic issue for the state, we wanted to take a deeper look into which schools did the best job of retaining students," wrote Flybridge Capital partner Jeff Bussgang in an August 2016 blog post.

Bussgang found that some colleges breed more graduates who tend to stay local, especially those with high numbers of students who were born and raised in Massachusetts. For example, nearly 60 percent of Bentley University and Northeastern University graduates remained in the Greater Boston area after graduation, while only about 20 percent of Harvard and MIT graduates remained local after graduating, according to the report, which culled location data from LinkedIn for more than 1.1 million Massachusetts college graduates.

According to another study, Boston was found to have the largest so-called "brain drain" out of 40 cities in the country, with more than 17,200 people with tech-focused degrees having left the city between 2011 and 2015, based on a July 2016 report by commercial real estate firm CBRE Group. The city that added the most tech workers over the same period was San Francisco, with a gain of about 89,600 people, according to the report.

Statistics aside, there are countless employees, businesses, entrepreneurs and graduates who firmly believe that Boston is the best place in the U.S. to build a career. And that belief is likely to become more widespread as more companies follow in the footsteps of General Electric, one of the largest companies the country, which recently chose Boston as the permanent home of its new headquarters.

> Statistics aside, there are countless employees, businesses, entrepreneurs and graduates who firmly believe that Boston is the best place in the U.S. to build a career.

Entrepreneur Nicole Sahin, for example, made a conscious decision in 2012 to choose Greater Boston as the home of her successful company, Globalization Partners. Originally from St. Louis, Sahin worked in Silicon Valley for years before deciding to start her own human resources technology company. She chose the Boston area over other tech-savvy cities in the U.S. part because of its rich history. The cobblestone streets and centuries-old monuments and educational institutions signaled to her that the city has been a pioneer of innovation throughout the ages.

"If you think a city has a soul, Boston has a social contract through history to be an agent of change," Sahin said, adding that the city was the birthplace of mass transportation and public schools, and was also the epicenter of the abolitionist movement.

At the heart of Boston's rich history of social change are the people who made it happen. And the city continues to breed those innovators, many of whom are becoming pioneers in their respective industries, from biotech to finance and particularly technology. Virtual reality, machine learning, artificial intelligence and cybersecurity are all sectors that Boston has a strong foothold in, with some of the most ardent technologists in the country inventing new technologies in those spaces.

For Sahin, it was the grit and intellectual nature of the people she met in Boston that kept her grounded in the city.

"I love Silicon Valley, but the people here are smarter, culturally," said Sahin, who grew her company's annual revenue to about $18 million in four years. "They're edgier, they don't give you any excuse to not be your best and your brightest at every moment. Each person is continuously pushing you forward."

For many people, including Sahin, Boston gives newcomers to the city an unparalleled chance to create a vast network of influential mentors and friends in a relatively short period of time. That might be due to the fact that geographically, Boston is tiny compared to other global cities of its stature, covering a total of 48 square miles. Neighboring Cambridge, home to MIT and Harvard, covers about 16 square miles. Size gives Boston a huge advantage when it comes to making important career connections that will last a lifetime.

That's certainly what recent college graduates like startup enthusiast Casey Hogan have found. A native of Rhode Island, Hogan graduated from Northeastern University in 2015 with a bachelor's degree in business administration, entrepreneurial and small business operations. During college and after graduating, she worked at several early-stage companies where she formed invaluable relationships with influential people in the Boston startup scene, including C.A. Webb, the former executive director of the New England Venture Capital Association.

After spending six months as an intern at a startup in San Francisco, she toyed with the idea of living there after school. But Boston called her back. "My network was bigger here and I knew it was going to be a lot easier to find a job here because I had a lot of people behind me, helping me," she said.

Hogan is now the community manager at a Boston-based co-working space for food-related startups called The Food Loft, and her decision to stay in Boston is constantly reaffirmed. Boston has a collaborative mentality. There's a willingness to help each other out, whether it's helping someone navigate the complex world of entrepreneurship or helping someone find a job.

"I have food entrepreneurs come up to me and say, 'I just learned all about distributing alcohol in the U.S. and if you know of anybody that needs help with this, let me know,'" she said.

That collaborative nature is also what makes the important people in Boston

— the venture capitalists, CEOs, founders and experts — receptive to cold calls and coffee meetings. That, more than anything, might be the best and most crucial way to begin building a network of people you can learn from.

"It's a lot easier to get in front of influencers here. It's easier to get in front of VCs and people who are running companies," said Amy Spurling, one of Boston's preeminent chief financial officers. "There's a lot more tolerance for people interested in what somebody else is building and what they can learn from it, and there's less ego."

Originally from northern California, Spurling moved to Boston in the late 1990s, chiefly because she could get around the city without a car, she almost always felt safe, and she was only a six-hour flight away from Europe.

Since then, she's built a successful career that has included spending more than a decade leading companies to acquisition. As the former CFO of Jana, she was most recently responsible for helping close a $57 million fundraising round for the company, a Boston-based mobile tech startup.

Spurling undoubtedly worked hard to earn every bit of her success, but some of the credit was due to the opportunities that Boston afforded her. When it comes to building a career, Boston's size matters, she said.

"Boston is a very major U.S. city, but it's a very manageable city," she said. "Once you start getting a little bit of momentum, depending on what sector you're in, you can make a name for yourself much more quickly than you could if you were in Silicon Valley."

Boston's geography of innovation and money management

Business is everywhere in the greater Boston area, but it has several notable, concentrated centers of world-class activity:

Kendall Square: Home to biotech and tech giants, and adjacent to MIT in Cambridge, Kendall Square may be the most concentrated innovation center in the country. Among the many companies and institutions with headquarters or offices there are Akamai, Amazon, Biogen, Genzyme, Google, Pegasystems, the Broad Institute and Novartis. Kendall Square also is the home of the Cambridge Innovation Center, a co-working space for startups that now has eight locations, including Boston, Miami and St. Louis.

Longwood Medical Area: An unmatched number of medical institutions populate the Longwood Medical Area, which is near the Fenway neighborhood and Simmons and Emmanuel colleges. Boston Children's Hospital, Brigham and Women's Hospital, Dana Farber Cancer Institute, and Harvard Medical School are among the prominent medical centers there. An estimated 46,000 people work in the area either administering or supporting medical care.

The Financial District: As the name implies, the Financial District, a swath of downtown Boston, is home to many financial services firms, including State Street Corp., Eaton Vance, Putnam Investments, and Bank of America's Boston operations (interestingly, Fidelity moved its headquarters from its longtime location on Devonshire Street to a location on Summer Street just past the fringe of the Financial District). Many of Boston's top law firms are located there as well, including WilmerHale and Mintz Levin. Many startups have poured into the area, giving it a growing tech feel, where they sometimes find relatively reasonable rents.

The Innovation District: Also known as the Seaport, many tech companies and accounting and law firms have gravitated across the channel to former warehouse buildings and new office buildings in the booming region broadly named the Innovation District. Local biotech giant Vertex's move to a new office building in the area helped signal a new era of branding Boston as an innovation center, and MassChallenge, the startup incubator, helped cement the region's new identity. Many tech firms have flooded in, including fast-growing public tech company LogMeIn. Most recently, General Electric chose the area for its new headquarters.

Route 128: Once dubbed "America's Technology Highway," Route 128, which circles north, west, and south of the Boston area, became an economic driver for the region after it was built in the 1950s. Many large tech firms and start-ups are located on the 65-mile highway, which stretches from Gloucester in the north to Braintree in the south. Among the bigger companies that have recently expanded their footprint along the route are TripAdvisor (Needham), AstraZeneca and VistaPrint (Waltham).

The Boston economy — by the numbers

Greater Boston population: **4.73 million** *(up 7.8 percent since 2000)*	Massachusetts population: **6.794 million** *(up 38 percent since 2000)*	Population growth in the city of Boston, 2010-2015: **38,204** *(total population 667,137)*
Total employment in Massachusetts: **3.49 million**	Massachusetts unemployment rate, October 2016: **3.3%**	Metropolitan Boston unemployment rate, July 2015: **2.4%**
Massachusetts average weekly wage, first quarter of 2015: **$1,341** *($69,732 annually)*	Average weekly wage, Boston, first quarter of 2015: **$1,909** *($99,268 annually)*	Number of businesses in Massachusetts with at least one employee: **206,599** *(as of March 2016)*
Number of businesses in Massachusetts with over 1,000 employees: **239** *(as of March 2016)*	Number of families earning over $1 million in Massachusetts in 2014: **15,273**	Percentage of families below poverty level, Massachusetts, 2015: **11.5%**
Total number of college students in Massachusetts (2013): **594,000**	Number of college students within the city of Boston: **150,000**	Boston residential population who are students: **16.5%**

Percentage of Boston's population between the ages of 20 and 34: **35%**	Percentage of Massachusetts residents (over 25 years old) with a bachelor's degree or higher: **39.4%**	Percentage of Boston residents (over 25 years old) with a bachelor's degree or higher: **43.9%**
Massachusetts 4-year college graduates' average student debt (2014): **$29,038**	Foreign college students in Massachusetts: **55,447**	Average rent for an apartment in Boston, end of 2015 (source: Reis): **$2,010**
Number of Boston apartments added to supply, 2014-2015 **10,800**	Number of Massachusetts jobs added in construction, Oct. 2015-Oct. 2016: **10,200**	Number of Massachusetts jobs added in financial services: Oct. 2015-Oct. 2016: **4,000**
Number of Massachusetts jobs added in professional, scientific, technical services: Oct. 2015-Oct. 2016: **18,100**	Amount invested in Massachusetts startups, 2014: **$7.42 billion**	Number of Massachusetts jobs added in restaurants and hotels, Oct. 2015-Oct. 2016: **6,100**
Overseas visitors to Boston, 2015: **1,609,000**	Number of visitors to Boston from China, 2015: **208,000**	Estimated amount to bring the MBTA into a "a state of good repair": **$7.3 billion**

PART ONE

Tech and the life sciences — companies, people, and trends

Fascinating startups and the venture capital behind them

Robots with sensors that make them human-like. Fuel produced from sunlight and carbon dioxide. Technology to enable self-driving taxis. These are among many world-changing technologies that are being brought to market by Boston-area startups.

The Boston-area economy's amazing array of tech startups has few rivals in the country. (Silicon Valley, of course, stands out as the major competitor). Venture capital firms poured some $8 billion into about 700 Massachusetts startups in 2015 and $3.7 billion in 322 startups as of August 2016, the majority of them located in Cambridge and Boston.

Massachusetts continues to cultivate an image of world-class innovation, particularly with the rapid emergence of the Innovation District, an area in the South Boston waterfront that includes the new Fort Point headquarters of General Electric Co., which has become a magnet for startups and other companies that want to do business with them. But there are no strict geographic limitations to where entrepreneurs are building their companies, although it's fair to say that there's been a gravitational pull away from the suburbs to the urban areas where the young talent wants to reside.

Here are the hottest startup clusters in the Greater Boston startup scene:

Big data & analytics

As humans, businesses and Internet-connected devices continue to produce vast amounts of data, demand continues to grow for startups that offer technologies to help make sense of the data and leverage those technologies as tools for growth. The term "big data" was coined only recently but the theory has been around for decades. It refers to the massive amounts of data being siphoned from objects connected to the Internet, and the way in which researchers and scientists analyze and make use of the data.

As more data is being siphoned from objects connected to the Internet — from phones to watches and light bulbs — the need for experts to analyze and make sense of it will only increase. Massachusetts is home to perhaps the most preeminent scholar in big data — serial entrepreneur and computer scientist Michael Stonebraker, who won the 2015 Turing Award, considered by many in the field to be the equivalent of the Nobel Prize for computer science. Since 2013, the amount of private investment that has flowed into big data companies in Massachusetts has topped $2.4 billion, according to a 2016 report from the Massachusetts Technology Collaborative. Between 2013 and 2016, more than 50 new data-focused companies have sprung up in the Bay State. The total number of Massachusetts companies specializing in data science related endeavors is more than 500, according to a 2015 report by the University of Massachusetts.

Examples of big data startups quickly gaining traction *(funding numbers as of August 2016):*

About 500 Massachusetts companies are currently working on data science-related endeavors.

Tamr, a Cambridge-based big data analytics startup founded in 2013, analyzes hundreds and thousands of data sources and applies advanced algorithms and machine learning to "unleash" the power of a company's data, according to the company. Total funding to date for the company is more than $42 million and its investors include high-profile names such as Hewlett Packard Ventures, Thomson Reuters and MassMutual Ventures, as well as NEA and Google Ventures.

VoltDB, a Bedford-based big data startup founded in 2009, offers what the company says is "the world's fastest operational database." The technology aims to help businesses capture, analyze and optimize real-time data that could ultimately lead to increases in their revenues. The company has now raised a total of $31.3 million and will use the newest investment to extend its in-memory database to power "the next wave of real-time, fast data-driven applications."

Experfy, a startup headquartered at Harvard's Innovation Launch Lab, connects enterprise-level companies looking to launch data science projects with the top data scientists in the world. Ultimately, the startup aims to revolutionize big-data consulting by offering an online marketplace to hire data scientists for consulting work on demand. Backed by less than $1 million, this budding startup is also trying to fill a gap in the demand for data scientists, which is growing by the thousands in Massachusetts.

Cybersecurity

Massachusetts has made a name for itself as a hotbed for businesses in the cybersecurity space. With high-profile data breaches impacting enterprise-level businesses like Target and Home Depot, smaller companies are beginning to recognize the need for security solutions to combat cyber hackers and thwart cyber threats. In fact, cybersecurity has become such a hot industry in the state that 34 companies in Massachusetts were named among the world's 500 most innovative cybersecurity firms, according to a report released in August 2016. "I've never seen more investment in the security space in my 20 years in the business as I'm seeing right now," said Arthur W. Coviello Jr., formerly the executive chairman of RSA, the security division of Hopkinton-based data storage giant EMC, in an interview with the Boston Business Journal in 2015. Fledgling startups in this space include Cambridge-based BitSight

> "I've never seen more investment in the security space in my 20 years in the business as I'm seeing right now."
> — Arthur W. Coviello Jr.

Technologies, which rates businesses on their cybersecurity performance, and Ireland-born SaltDNA, a startup now headquartered in Cambridge, which offers a mobile app that allows users to text message, call and access data from a mobile device with complete privacy. In 2015, the only two Massachusetts technology companies to go public were both in the cybersecurity sector: Rapid7 and Mimecast. Now, other later-stage cybersecurity firms are thinking of following suit. Among them: Burlington-based Veracode and Waltham-based Carbon Black.

Examples of cybersecurity startups quickly gaining traction (*funding numbers as of August 2015*):

Sqrrl, a Cambridge-based big data analytics startup, recently unveiled a new software aimed at detecting and responding to cybersecurity threats. The company says it makes software to uncover hidden patterns, trends and links in data. Founded in 2012, the company's customers include several undisclosed Fortune 500 companies and large government agencies. Total investor funding to date for the company is $14.2 million, with investors including Rally Ventures, Atlas Venture and Matrix Partners.

Threat Stack, a Boston-based IT security firm that was founded in 2012, has gained a significant increase in customers as demand for its cloud-based security services has skyrocketed. Threat Stack offers infrastructure monitoring and threat intelligence applications for companies including artificial intelligence software firm Nara Logics and cloud services company Acquia. Threat Stack is backed by $26.6 million in venture capital funding with investors including Accomplice and .406 Ventures.

Cybereason, a Cambridge-based cybersecurity firm whose founder was formerly with the Israeli Intelligence Corps, is growing with $88 million in venture capital funding since its founding in 2012. Cybereason's software can analyze up to eight million events per second to discover elements of a cyber attack including its timeline, root cause and malicious software involved, all in real time. Earlier this spring, Lockheed Martin, one of Cybereason's customers and investors, announced it will be providing Cybereason's technology to its Fortune 100 clients.

Cleantech

Companies in the clean technology space in Massachusetts are gaining enormous traction. That's partly due to the influence of the unique Somerville-based cleantech startup incubator program Greentown Labs, whose startups have raised more than $100 million since 2011, and cleantech organizations such as the New England Water Innovation Network and the Massachusetts Clean Energy Center. Massachusetts government is also recognizing the importance of these companies in the startup ecosystem:

Gov. Charlie Baker's administration announced in May 2015 it would make $800,000 in funding available for innovative water-technology projects throughout the state. Some of the state funding will be used to establish a testing network for companies interested in testing their technologies. Innovations in water technology are gaining particular momentum in Massachusetts, with about 100 companies in the state representing a $1.7 billion water technology industry. The water technology cluster has contributed to the creation of more than 12,300 direct and indirect jobs in Massachusetts and a $2.8 billion economic impact, according to a 2015 report released by the Massachusetts Clean Energy Center. The Bay State has also become a hub for innovations in lighting technology, with energy-efficient and "smart" lighting innovations including Boston-based companies Digital Lumens and ByteLight, acquired in 2015 by Acuity Brands Inc.

Examples of cleantech startups quickly gaining traction (*funding numbers as of August 2016*):

Though Boston-based solar energy company **Nexamp** has been around since 2007, the company scored a $30 million infusion of cash from Mitsubishi Corp.'s energy subsidiary in August 2016. The subsidiary, called Diamond Generating Corp., will help Nexamp build and operate commercial-level solar energy projects around the country. Among Nexamp's solar projects are a 2.3 megawatt, 12-acre community solar project at Massachusetts ski resort Jiminy Peak, which is expected to help the resort decrease its energy use by up to 90 percent.

MIT-born **Accion Systems**, a Cambridge-based maker of electric propulsion systems for satellites, is currently participating in the Somerville-based cleantech incubator program Greentown Labs. The company's cleantech play is developing liquid ion sources for micro-propulsion systems in satellites — systems that could one day be used in small satellites to provide constant earth imagery to track the growth of corn crops to better predict their yields to better monitor natural disaster, or to provide global Internet coverage. The company is backed by about $10 million from investors including FF Science, a seed-stage investment firm that spun out of Silicon Valley's Founders Fund last year.

Joule Unlimited: What if a combination of sunlight, carbon dioxide, water and specially engineered bacteria could produce ethanol to power cars and jets? That's the promise of Joule, which has the potential to disrupt the conventional fossil fuel industry with a technology that can create fuel in many locations. Based in Bedford, Mass., the company has raised $190 million.

1366 Technologies: A maker of solar power wafers, the building blocks for solar cells, 1366 is looking to drive down costs in an industry that has seen many other solar companies fail. Based in Bedford, Mass., it has raised $81.4 million.

Robotics

From robots that can read bedtime stories to drones that can take high-quality photos and video to robots that work alongside manufacturers in warehouses, Massachusetts is home to dozens of consumer- and enterprise-focused robotics firms. Notable big businesses in the robotics industry are Bedford-based publicly traded tech company iRobot, maker of the Roomba, the popular robotic vacuum cleaner, to Boston Dynamics, which was acquired by Google in 2013 and makes eerily powerful humanoid robots meant to work alongside military members. According to a 2013 study by the Massachusetts Technology Leadership Council, the Bay State is home to more than 150 robotics companies serving 11 markets, with more than 35 robotics research and development programs across 18 institutions.

Examples of robotics startups gaining traction:

Weston-based **Jibo Inc.** struck crowdfunding gold in 2014 when it set out to raise $100,000 on crowdfunding website Indiegogo. Instead, the company raised a whopping $2.3 million from more than 5,500 backers. In early 2015, the company looked to venture capitalists for more funding, securing about $60 million and landing a former executive of Burlington-based publicly traded software firm Nuance Communications as its CEO. The robot, also named Jibo, is billed as "the world's first social robot." At six pounds, Jibo is capable of many tasks including acting as a personal assistant and an "on-demand cameraman," picking up on cues like movement, speech commands and smiles to know when someone's posing for a picture. Founded by MIT scientist Cynthia Breazeal in 2012, Jibo Inc. is one of the fastest-growing early-stage robotics companies in the state.

> At six pounds in weight, Jibo is capable of many tasks including acting as a personal assistant and an "on-demand cameraman."

Helen Greiner, one of the most influential roboticists in Massachusetts, founded Danvers-based flying robot-maker **CyPhy Works** in 2008. The company in May launched its first consumer product: a high-quality, easy-to-use drone that users can control via a mobile app. CyPhy Works has raised $12.5 million in venture capital funding to date (August 2015) and is hoping to capitalize on hobbyists' enthusiasm for drones.

Founded in 2008, Boston-based **Rethink Robotics** is the maker of two robot products named Baxter and Sawyer that work alongside workers in manufacturing plants. Backed by about $100 million in current funding to date (August 2015) with investors including GE Ventures and Goldman Sachs, the company aims to help alleviate challenges with labor shortages in geographies such as China.

Artificial Intelligence

Artificial intelligence has long been thought of as synonymous with the underlying technology behind robots that can mimic — or someday surpass the intellectual capacity and efficiency of — humans. During the past few years, the Bay State has seen a surge of activity in the thriving area of artificial intelligence, from MIT-born nuTonomy's work on self-driving taxis to Boston tech firm Neurala using AI to help drones recognize objects in their way. But AI is not only restricted to the robotics industry. Researchers at Cambridge-based IBM Security, for example, are using the fundamentals of artificial intelligence to train computer software to digest and understand thousands of documents on cybercrime. In that scenario, the hope is that the software, called IBM Watson, could eventually become one of the most powerful technologies available to companies in the global effort to thwart hackers. Startups in the marketing and human resources industries are also leveraging AI in their efforts to become more efficient in their respective domains. In fact, AI-related startups have become so abundant that a Boston-based venture capital firm called Glasswing Ventures was developed in July 2016 with the goal of investing in startups that leverage AI. That firm is currently looking to raise $150 million to invest in startups.

Here are some of the Bay State's most promising startups figuring out novel ways to use artificial intelligence:

nuTonomy Inc is a Cambridge-based startup founded by MIT graduates that recently landed $16 million in venture capital funding to test software for self-driving taxis, mainly in Singapore. The company has a goal of deploying its self-driving taxis in about two years.
Total funding: $20 million
Investors: Highland Capital Partners, Fontinalis Partners, Signal Ventures

Ava is a Woburn startup with a lofty mission for users interested in eating healthier and losing weight. Its goal: let users take a photo of their meal, send it to the company via text message, and get health information from

nutritionists and AI software. The company is in its very early stages, but could eventually compete with well-funded traditional food-logging and weight-loss mobile apps like Boston-based Lose It!
Total funding: $3 million
Investors include: DCM Ventures, Khosla Ventures, Innovation Endeavors

A Franklin tech firm called **Interactions** landed a $56 million infusion of cash in August 2016 to bolster its work on artificial intelligence software that could someday replace the need for customer service representatives. The technology is intended to improve automated customer-service software for phone calls and text messages.
Total funding: $167 million
Investors: Revolution Growth, NewSpring Capital and Comcast Ventures

'Unicorns' and other top-funded local startups
(Funding numbers as of August, 2016)

A few landmark funding deals were struck during the first half of 2015, valuing startups that are just a few years old at hundreds of millions — if not billions — of dollars. In the jargon-heavy tech world, startups that have a valuation of $1 billion or more are called "unicorns." Several early-stage companies have earned "unicorn" status during the past few years because of large funding deals, including DraftKings and SimpliVity.

Here are examples of some of the Boston-area's most well funded startups:

DraftKings, a Boston-based online daily fantasy sports startup announced in November 2016 it intended to merge with its New York-based rival, FanDuel. The object of controversy and regulatory scrutiny around fantasy sports, DraftKings's investors include: Fox Sports, Major League Baseball
Total funding to date: $630 million since 2011

SimpliVity, headquartered in Westborough, makes an IT appliance system for data centers, looking to transform an $80 billion server market
Most recent funding round amount: $175 million in March, 2015 Investors include: Accel Partners, CRV
Total funding to date: $276.5 million since 2009

Infinidat, an Israeli company with its U.S. headquarters in Needham, is a data storage company founded by a former executive at Hopkinton-based data storage giant EMC, one of the largest tech firms in the state.
Most recent funding round amount: $150 million in April, 2015 Investors include: TPG Growth
Total funding to date: $230 million since 2011

Altiostar Networks, headquartered in Tewksbury, is the maker of technology that makes it possible for cell phone carriers to more efficiently send data wirelessly.
Most recent funding amount: $70 million in January, 2015 Investors include: Cisco Systems and Excelestar Ventures
Total funding to date: $150 million since 2011

Kaminario, headquartered in Newton, is a data storage company that aims to compete directly with publicly traded tech giants like EMC. Most recent funding amount: $68 million in January, 2015
Investors include: Sequoia Capital, Pitango Venture Capital and Globespan Capital Partners
Total funding to date: $153 million since 2010

Turbonomics, a cloud technology company headquartered in Boston that was formerly known as VMturbo. Most recent funding amount: $50 million in January, 2015 Investors include: ICONIQ Capital, Bain Capital
Total funding to date: $77.5 million since 2009

Interactions, a Franklin-based tech firm that offers a virtual assistant technology aimed at improving conversations between customers and customer service representatives.
Most recent funding amount: $56 million
Investors include: AOL founder Steve Case's Revolution Growth, NewSpring Capital and Comcast Ventures
Total funding to date: $167 million since 2002

Fuze, formerly known as ThinkingPhones, landed $112 million in new funding earlier this year that will be used for expansion. The company offers cloud-based communications services including video and voice calling for businesses like IdeaPaint and Cambridge Innovation Center.
Investors include: Summit Partners, Bessemer Venture Partners, Technology

Crossover Ventures
Total funding to date: More than $200 million since 2006

Nantero, headquartered in Woburn, is a semiconductor company with the mission of commercializing a novel digital memory product that could eventually replace memory in cellphones, digital cameras and tablets.
Most recent funding amount: $35 million in March, 2015 and $9.5 million in August, 2015
Investors include: Globespan Capital Partners, Charles River Ventures and Draper Fisher Jurvetson
Total funding to date: $82 million since 2001

Onshape, headquartered in Cambridge, specializes in computer-aided design (CAD)
Most recent funding amount: $25 million, April, 2016
Investors include: New Enterprise Associates, North Bridge Venture Partners, and Commonwealth Capital, Andreessen Horowitz
Total funding to date: $169 million

Other startups of note
(Funding numbers as of August, 2016):

Indigo: An agriculture technology startup that kept a low profile in Boston surprised the local innovation sector by raising a whopping $100 million in venture funding from Alaska Permanent Fund and Flagship Ventures. The company now has about $156 million in funding to date and is pouring its latest influx of cash into research and development, to fine-tune new technologies that could end up revolutionizing the cotton industry.

One startup has created a special coating that aims to change how we experience condiments and other products.

Circle: Circle has pivoted from a startup with a mission to spur mainstream adoption for the digital currency Bitcoin to a well-funded startup aimed at allowing users to easily send and receive payment. Founded by serial entrepreneur Jeremy Allaire, Circle is the maker of a mobile app built on blockchain technology that garnered $60 million in new funding in June. Investors include Beijing-based IDG Capital Partners and Beijing search engine giant Baidu.

Desktop Metal: This Lexington-based startup is on a mission to create an affordable metal 3-D printer. To that end, it has raised a whopping $52 million in investor funding in about a year. According to its website, Desktop Metal is "the effortless way to go from 3D (computer-aided design) to robust metal parts." Its 3D build complex parts "beautifully and at a price that makes it attainable by every design and manufacturing team."

Happier: This Boston-based company has produced a web platform and app designed to help make people happier. The company's products "encourage people to collect and share everyday happy moments, and do more of what makes them happier," according to its website. The startup, created by Russian immigrant Nataly Kogan, has raised $3.2 million.

LiquiGlide: With technology out of MIT, this startup aims to change how we experience condiments. Ten percent of condiments are wasted; but not with this company's spray coating. The Cambridge company has attracted $7.1 million in funding.

Fascinating apps on the Boston app scene

The Boston area has an ambitious app development scene. Here are a few of the top players:

FitnessKeeper, based in Boston, is the maker of the RunKeeper app, which tracks users' fitness regiments. It reportedly has over 40 million users. The company was bought in February 2016 by Japanese fitness equipment company Asics Corp. for $85 million.

Ovuline makes the Ovia Fertility app, which takes credit for helping 175,000 couples get pregnant (as of October 2014).

Foodler, a food ordering and delivery app, has gained traction in a crowded field of dining-related apps.

Lose it!, a weight-loss app that tracks calorie consumption, was created by FitNow and reportedly has over 24 million users as of March, 2015.

The startup incubators

Boston's growing startup ecosystem continues to spawn new incubators that provide cheap or free space for young companies along with expertise from experienced entrepreneurs to help them along.

Among the most prominent incubators are:

MassChallenge, located in South Boston, runs an accelerator program and a startup competition, and organizes training and networking for its participants.

TechStars is a national accelerator program backed by venture capitalists and other investors and has locations in seven cities including Boston. The Boston program boasts 69 active alumni startups, including Localytics.

For a list of incubators and accelerators in Massachusetts, see this list created by the Massachusetts Tech Collaborative.
masstech.org/innovation-ecosystem/innovation-economy-resources/incubators-and-accelerators-o

The venture capitalists

Venture capitalists, or VCs, are the lubricant in the engine of the startup economy. They gather investment funds, often from institutions such as pension funds and college endowments, and take partial ownership stakes in the startups, sometimes joining the board of directors of the startup to help steer the strategic direction of the company. Many startups fail, but VCs sometimes receive astronomical returns on their investments that more than make up for the startups that fold. For example, Spark Capital invested about $10 million during fairly early stages of Twitter growth, getting about 5 percent of the company. At the time of Twitter's IPO, that stake was valued at about $900 million. Below are some of the most active local venture capital firms.

Atlas Venture is among the most active investors in local startups, and its roster of portfolio companies includes DraftKings and DataXu.

Flagship Ventures specializes in biotech and clean tech, and its portfolio includes Joule.

Highland Capital Partners has invested in mobile payment company LevelUp, among many other local startups.

Polaris Partners invests in health care and tech startups and is an investor in 1366 Technologies.

Charles River Ventures, one of the original VC firms in Boston, has invested in Rethink Robotics and SimpliVity.

Flybridge Capital is an investor in Digital Lumens and Jibo.

Spark Capital is looking for more home runs after Twitter. Local portfolio companies include RunKeeper, Cybereason and fintech startup Quantopian.

Women & startups

Statistics on women in technology and female-founded technology companies raising venture capital funding are, in a word, dismal. According to a 2014 Babson College study, 2.7 percent of venture capital-funded companies had a woman CEO, and the total number of female partners at venture firms has dropped from 10 percent in 1999 to 6 percent now. Out of the approximately 45 publicly-traded technology companies in Massachusetts, only two are led by women: Care.com's Sheila Lirio Marcelo and Mary Puma of Axcelis Technologies. (Constant Contact's Gail Goodman was the third until her company agreed to be acquired in November, 2015.) There's a significant dearth in women in technology and venture capital in the Bay State, and both men and women recognize it. However, significant strides are being made in this area that will serve as a foundation for future improvements. In 2015, the first women in venture capital summit was held in Boston with the mission of highlighting women-led startups and increasing awareness of the current venture-funding gap that exists for women-led businesses. Several Boston-area entrepreneurs also have made it their mission to boost the visibility of female entrepreneurs and technologists that are in the state. For example, a Woburn-based website called Women Innovation was created in mid-2015 with a mission to allow event organizers to search for experienced female professionals to be speakers on panels. And in 2014, a Boston-based software startup called WomenLEAD launched with the mission of matching female professionals with executives that act as advisers to help fulfill career goals.

In 2015, the first women in venture capital summit was held in Boston with the mission of highlighting women-led startups.

The number of young female entrepreneurs in the Boston area is also beginning to rise. About 44 percent of the 128 startups in the 2015 MassChallenge startup accelerator program, headquartered in Boston, have at least one female founder — up from 31 percent in 2012, and a record for the program. Industry analysts peg the percentage of startups overall with at least one female founder at about 10 percent.

People to know, among many, in the startup world

David Chang

Chang is the former chief operating officer of PayPal Media Network. He spearheaded the Boston-based startup accelerator program PayPal StartTank (which merged with Boston-based accelerator program MassChallenge in 2014). Known in the entrepreneurial community as a "startup evangelist," Chang has invested in numerous early-stage ventures including Boston-based adtech startup Inmoji and Sonation, a Boston-based music technology company. Chang was named executive chairman of a startup Feelter, which is developing an online shopping tool, in November 2016

Rudina Seseri

Seseri is one of the only technology-focused venture capitalists in the state who is female, and at 38 years old, she's certainly the youngest. A former partner at Cambridge-based venture firm Fairhaven Capital, Seseri's portfolio includes successful startups including Jibo Inc., the Weston-based maker of a social robot that landed about $60 million in investor funding in two years. Now, Rudina is the head of another venture capital fund, Glasswing Ventures, which invests in startups that leverage artificial intelligence technology. Hailing from Albania, Seseri is a graduate of Wellesley College and Harvard Business School.

Paul English

English is the co-founder of online travel website Kayak, acquired by Connecticut-based Priceline for about $1.8 billion. He left Kayak in 2014 to co-found Blade, a Boston-based consumer-tech startup incubator, and then in 2016 after his noncompete agreement with Kayak ran out, he founded travel tech startup Lola.

Chris Lynch

Known for his unusually candid and sometimes irreverent nature, Lynch is one of the most outspoken venture capitalists in Boston's startup world.

Serial entrepreneur Paul English's advice: 'The team you're with is more important than the company'

Paul English is something of a legend in the Boston tech scene. The University of Massachusetts graduate co-founded several companies including the successful travel website Kayak Software Corp., which he sold to Priceline for $1.8 billion in 2012. He was recently the subject of the book "A Truck Full of Money" by Tracy Kidder, which chronicled his somewhat serendipitous rise to success while battling bipolar disorder. English is heavily involved in the Boston startup scene, especially nowadays, as the founder and CEO of the early-stage travel startup Lola.

Paul English *(John Davenport photo)*

Q: What do employers look for in candidates when they're hiring at a startup?

A: I think extra curricular activities are really important. Seeing that someone has been entrepreneurial already, seeing that someone has already started a project, is important. It can be anything, but it's important to show that they participated in creating a new organization, it could be a nonprofit or a club they created or a small business they're running out of their dorm room. You want to make sure somebody really has an interest in entrepreneurship. I like kids that have mowed lawns more than kids that work at the grocery store, because when you're mowing lawns, you have to service each customer and sell them, and make money, and do the transactions on your own schedule.

Q: What's important to keep in mind when looking for a job at a startup?

A: I lecture at MIT and UMass a lot, and sometimes students ask me, should I join a large company like Kayak or a new startup that doesn't have funding yet? To me, the criteria you should use to decide between those is to figure out who are the two or three people you're actually going to spend time with, and whichever of those companies has the strongest people, go with that company. For your first job out of college, the team you're with is more important than the company, so pick the team first. I also recommend that kids work in a structured and unstructured environment; both are important for becoming an entrepreneur.

Q: Are there any advantages of working at a startup?

A: If you're working at a venture-backed startup and you have a really good CEO and set of co-founders, many times they can recruit stronger people more than a big, tired company can. Sometimes you have much stronger colleagues to work with that are more entrepreneurial and driven. A small startup doesn't have much structure, so you'll get to define your job and you'll get to work on things that aren't assigned to you. There's a little bit more flexibility to make your own space. At a startup it's the norm that people can try different types of jobs.

As the former CEO of database-software firm Vertica Systems, he came on board when the Billerica-based company was out of cash and ensnared in two lawsuits. Within a year, the company was acquired by Hewlett-Packard Co. for nearly $400 million. His investments span across several big data and cybersecurity-focused technologies including Boston-based cloud security firm ThreatStack and Cambridge-based big data analytics startup Sqrrl.

Michael Stonebraker

Serial entrepreneur Stonebraker is a researcher at MIT Computer Science and Artificial Intelligence Laboratory and the 2015 winner of the Turing Award, considered to be the "Nobel Prize for computer science." Known as the "big data forefather," Stonebraker has been working on the field of database management for four decades. He has co-founded several Massachusetts companies in the big data space, including Bedford-based operational database company VoltDB, Cambridge-based big data startup Tamr and Billerica-based Vertica Systems, bought by Hewlett-Packard for $340 million in 2011.

Jean Hammond

Hammond made a name for herself as an angel investor in 2000 when she bet on car sharing company Zipcar — which paid off. A graduate of MIT's Sloan School of Management, Hammond sits on several boards of companies including Wellesley-based real-time marketing company InStream Media and Boston-based lingerie brand Peach Underneath. She's also responsible for helping create the Boston-based education technology startup accelerator program LearnLaunchX.

Jodi Goldstein

As managing director of the Harvard Innovation Lab, Goldstein has helped dozens of undergraduate startup founders turn their ideas from concept to reality. She also spearheaded a project called the Harvard Launch Lab, which offers annual co-working space and mentorship opportunities for 50 startups founded by Harvard alumni. An entrepreneur herself, Goldstein is the co-founder of a Somerville-based mobile app for wine called Drync.

Emily Reichert

As the executive director of Somerville-based cleantech startup incubator Greentown Labs, Reichert has helped significantly grow the state's cleantech presence. Under her leadership, Greentown Labs has become a model for other incubator programs in the cleantech space worldwide, and early-stage hardware startups have made important inroads with Massachusetts manufacturers because of an initiative to bring manufacturing jobs back to the Bay State. Since the incubator program was founded in 2011, Reichert has helped more than 75 startups secure about $100 million in total investor funding.

Maia Heymann

Heymann is one of the most well-known angel investors in the Boston area and has extensive experience in corporate finance, private equity, and venture capital. As the senior managing director of Converge Venture Partners, she has helped shape the startup investing group into a hybrid investment model: With a $26.5 million fund closed in 2014, the firm comprises about 60 active Boston-area investors who collectively invest in early-stage startups in the Boston area and also provide mentorship, expertise and connections for startup founders.

Diane Hessan

Hessan is the co-founder and chairwoman of Boston-based C Space, a global market research consultancy firm she ran for 15 years. In 2015, Hessan decided to switch career paths and become CEO of the Boston-based Startup Institute, which offers four curriculum programs for adults interested in entrepreneurship: web development, web design, technical marketing and sales and account management. She left her role at Startup Institute recently to work on an undisclosed project, but she's still a frequent speaker on tech panels and at startup events.

> Diane Hessan, a well-known tech leader, has become the CEO of the Boston-based Startup Institute.

Jeff Bussgang

Bussgang is a general partner at Flybridge Capital Partners and a senior lecturer at Harvard Business School. Along with weighing investments in many tech startups, Bussgang has ventured into the political realm, catalyzing the creation of a state-funded program called Global Entrepreneur in Residence that is designed to keep recently graduated international students from having to immediately return to their home countries.

So you want to join a startup?
Here are some ideas how

Working for a startup could be one of the most enriching experiences of your career, but you shouldn't take the decision to join one lightly. Don't be fooled by the allure of game rooms and beer o'clock Fridays. Those ping pong tables you see in the corner? Employees aren't using them. They're usually sleeping under them. "Be ready to work harder than you've worked before," says Jonathan Lacoste, the co-founder and president of Boston-based marketing technology firm Jebbit, which has been on a growth spree since the founders dropped out of college in 2011 to focus on the company full-time.

If you want to land a job at a startup, first, be honest with yourself. Do a self-audit. What are your biggest strengths, weaknesses, fears and ambitions? Entrepreneurs, recruiters and experts in the startup community all agree that successful employees of early-stage companies all possess one similar characteristic: they're scrappy. Employers see tenaciousness, determination and an aggressive, innovative spirit as huge upsides when filling a job. Those are also the same types of people who thrive in a fast-paced environment that's challenging and constantly changing — which is wildly different from the work environment at a job at a large, established corporation. Lacoste said the employees excel at Jebbit when they "embrace chaos."

A little bit of chaos and less red tape is what most people desire when they're considering leaving the confines of their cubicles at a corporate job and entering the startup world. That's what Rob Weeks was looking for after working at Blue Chip Boston-area companies like Raytheon and Bose. After spending four years working for those large corporations, he thought his mechanical engineering degree, analytical skills and innate sense of creativity could be put to better use. "I loved the idea of creative problem solving, but I hated sitting in a cube," he said. He saved some money and left the safety net of the corporate life to make networking a full-time job. He spent time at startup accelerators and programs like Boston-based hardware incubator

Bolt, attended various startup demo days, and went to the dozens of startup and tech networking events that are offered weekly in Boston. A few start-ups piqued his interest, but they didn't have open paid positions. Weeks was undeterred. Instead, he worked for free at various startups and identified himself as a contractor when he attended networking events. "It's scary not to get paid for a few months, but it allowed me to break in pretty easily into the startup world, and I met people I wouldn't have met otherwise," he said. After about three months, he landed a job at New York City-based co-working space firm WeWork and is now the regional manager of the Northeast division of the Young Entrepreneur Council. Aside from networking heavily, Weeks' advice for anyone looking for a job at a startup is to practice your pitch. "Your own personal brand is just as important as a company brand," he said.

Boston is a city where CEOs of Fortune 500 companies, venture capitalists and technology gurus are receptive to cold calls and emails. Recruiters advise job seekers to go straight to the source when looking for a job at a startup, and set up meetings with executives at companies that interest you. Just because startups don't have job openings listed on their website doesn't mean they're not actively hiring. "Express your interest in the company, and share how you think you could contribute to the team. Startups respect hustle, so be direct, and follow up," says Diana Martz, director of talent at Boston-based venture capital firm OpenView Ventures.

Martz, who specializes in helping find talented employees for the venture firm's portfolio companies, said it's not uncommon for prospective employees who have experience at larger companies to get passed over for startup jobs. That's because they're not viewed as scrappy enough to succeed on a smaller team with a smaller budget, or without a big brand name behind them, she said. "Overcome these objections by addressing them head on — in your cover letter, on your resume, and on your LinkedIn profile — and show what you have worked on individually as opposed to your team or department, and the metrics you've used to measure your success," she said.

Martz said the roles startups are looking to fill the most are in the departments of engineering and sales. Specific job titles that are in demand the most include: front-end software engineers, full stack software engineers, business development representatives, account executives and regional sales directors.

When you're past the networking stage and startups begin courting you, due diligence is key. Working at a startup is an investment, and one that could only be temporary, because statistics show that about 90 percent of startups fail. Startups differ vastly from one another in market, size, investor funding, maturity and culture, so it's important to get a sense of what it would be like working at one before you accept the job offer. Some of the happiest startup employees say they took their time to shadow a handful of companies like they'd shadow students at different colleges before deciding which one felt right. Spending a day learning, listening and asking questions can be the difference between landing at a job you're passionate about and working as a lackluster employee.

Working at a startup often gives employees the chance to take real, tangible ownership in a specific role. But be realistic and cautious when planning long-term. Ask yourself whether you'd still be grateful for the skills you learned and the projects you've helped execute at the company, even if the experience was temporary.

Resources

The Startup Institute
startupinstitute.com
This Boston-based organization offers an eight-week crash course for those looking to transition to the startup world and learn marketable skills. Four tracks are offered in the full-time course, ranging from web development to technical marketing. The program also offers part-time courses.

Eventbrite
eventbrite.com
Organizations that promote technology and startup networking events frequently post descriptions of their events on this website. Type "startups" and "Boston" in the search function sort the list by daily, weekly or monthly events.

WeWork
wework.com
This is a New York City-based co-working space firm that has two locations in Boston and is rapidly expanding. This model differs from other co-working spaces in the area (of which there are many) because of the community it

offers entrepreneurs. WeWork also hosts various events throughout the year that are open to the public.

TechHub
https://boston.techhub.com
This organization bills itself as a program that "creates spaces around the world for tech entrepreneurs to meet, work, learn and collaborate, and runs a load of great events, advice sessions and more." The organization often hosts networking events and demo days.

MITX
mitx.org
The Massachusetts Innovation and Technology Exchange offers monthly classes that are open to the public on the topics of innovation and entrepreneurship.

StartHub
starthub.org
In October 2015, the city of Boston unveiled StartHub, a homepage for tech entrepreneurs in Boston. It has listings of events, jobs, investors, workspaces and companies.

The Boston area's high-tech Goliaths — Large public companies, and some emerging ones

Some Boston startups grow up to become large, thriving enterprises whose market value, as measured by the amount its total stock is worth, well exceeds

$1 billion. This chapter will focus on the Boston area's roster of tech giants, publicly traded companies that employ many thousands of workers. Boston has a rich history of innovation, and it has succeeded in reinventing itself as a tech leader decade after decade.

Within the Boston region's high-tech cluster, there is significant diversification: defense, semiconductors, data storage, cybersecurity, and a wide array of specialized software and information technology companies. While Boston's many startups understandably generate excitement and receive a lot of media attention, some of Boston's more mature, larger tech companies continue to prosper in relative anonymity.

Raytheon: The granddaddy of Massachusetts high technology

No tech company in Massachusetts has evolved more effectively than **Raytheon**, one of the world's defense industry giants. In the 1920s, Raytheon invented the technology that helped make radios affordable for the mass market, went on to invent ship radar used in World War II, created guided missiles in the 1950s, and built the computer that guided Apollo 11 to the moon in 1969. Raytheon is now known for missile defense weaponry and technology, especially the Patriot missile, and it is working on the next generation of homeland security technology. The company employs over 61,000 people worldwide, and 11,000 in Massachusetts, making it one of the state's largest employers.

Raytheon plays an active role promoting science and technology in local schools and has internship programs to help fill its talent pipeline.

Beyond Raytheon: Mass. defense sector prospers

While the success of Raytheon has largely defined the Boston area defense industry, there are many prominent but much less celebrated players that are conducting research and developing various products to enhance the nation's defense. The Department of Defense awarded $8.6 billion to Massachusetts companies and institutions in its 2016 fiscal year and Raytheon received about 35 percent of those funds, leaving more than $5 billion for a wide assortment of entities, big and small. Although defense-related firms and institutions are inherently engineering-centric, like all large companies they have needs well beyond the core R&D function. Among the top companies.

MITRE: This federally funded nonprofit has a large campus in Bedford, Mass. and operates research centers for military and civil government agencies. It has over 7,600 employees worldwide, and 1,800 in Massachusetts.

Draper Labs is a large nonprofit research company, headquartered in Kendall Square, Cambridge, that specializes in developing technology for national security, health care, space exploration and energy. The company has about 1,200 employees in Cambridge.

MIT Lincoln Laboratory, based in Lexington, Mass. on the grounds of Hanscom Air Force Base, was founded in 1951 to conduct research to advance national security, including air and missile defense, space surveillance technology, tactical systems, biological and chemical defense, homeland protection, communications, cyber security, and information sciences. The organization employs approximately 1,700.

General Dynamics Mission Systems, a division of Virginia-based General Dynamics, operates a 130,000-square-foot facility in Dedham, Mass., as well as in Taunton, Mass. This unit focuses on what's called C4ISR systems (command, control, communications, computer, intelligence, surveillance and reconnaissance.)

Mercury Systems is a public technology company based in Chelmsford, Mass. with a focus on processing systems for the defense industry. It has over 950 employees worldwide.

Other significant recipients of defense dollars in Massachusetts include General Electric and its Lynn jet engine plant, with an estimated 2,800 employees. BAE Systems has several Massachusetts sites, as does defense giant Northrop Grumman.

The defense industry gravitates to Boston for the tech talent base as well as the startup culture, whose innovations are becoming more relevant to the defense industry as connectivity and data analytics become increasingly important technical advantages. Recognizing the potent market of the defense industry and other government agencies to the region's innovators, both big and small, Massachusetts Gov. Baker in partnership with MITRE launched the Massachusetts Innovation Bridge in early 2016. Led by Charlie Benway, its goal is to help build relationships between federal agencies and local companies and institutions.

Headquartered in Waltham, Raytheon also has facilities in Andover, Burlington, Tewksbury, and Marlborough, Mass. Annual revenue was about $23.25 billion in 2015. The company probably employs more engineers than any other Massachusetts company, and it is always in the hunt for new talent. The company plays an active role promoting science and technology in local schools and has internship programs to help create a pipeline of newly minted engineering grads.

EMC: Data storage leader evolves — and then is acquired

The enormous growth of computer data created a need to store it. **EMC Corp.**, one of Massachusetts' leading tech companies, reached a deal to be acquired by Dell in October 2015. EMC (now part of newly named Dell Technologies) was an early leader in data storage but eventually branched out into a variety of related niches, including cloud computing and Internet security software, but at its core remained a storage company. EMC was founded by Richard Egan and Roger Marino, college roommates at Northeastern, in 1979. It employed about 9,000 in

Massachusetts at the time of the merger, but it is truly an international company, deriving over 50 percent of its revenue from international sales. The implications of the Dell deal continue to unfold, but it almost never is a good thing in terms of job growth when a large local company is acquired by an out-of-state or international company.

Acquisitions had been critical to EMC's own growth. Among its largest purchases was VMware, a data visualization company, which has since been spun out into a very successful public company with $6 billion in annual revenue. EMC, however, at the time of its deal with Dell, still owned 80 percent of VMware. EMC acquired a successful local company, RSA Security, a leader in security software, in 2006, creating a foundation for its portfolio of data and Internet security products. In all, with its panoply of information technology offerings, EMC brought in $24.7 billion in revenue in 2015.

Chip makers, chip testers

The Boston area has a sizable, but relatively uncelebrated, semiconductor cluster. The "chips" that drive computing power, most popularly associated with companies like Intel (which has a significant research facility in Hudson, Mass.), are also used in an endless array of electronic equipment, and Boston area companies are generating billions in sales designing specialized semiconductor applications.

One of the oldest and most successful semiconductor companies is **Analog Devices**, which was founded in 1965 by two MIT grads, Ray Stata and Matthew Lorber. The company makes chips for all kinds of electronic equipment, including scientific instrumentation, industrial process controls, and audio and visual and automotive. One of its chips contributes to the electronic circuitry of the latest version of Apple's iPhone. Headquartered southwest of Boston in Norwood, Mass., Analog Devices had $3.4 billion in revenue in its 2015 fiscal year and employs about 9,600 people.

Another leading chip-making company in Greater Boston today is **Skyworks Solutions**, which was formed via a 2002 merger. Skyworks makes analog semiconductors — they're different in some key aspects from their digital cousins — used in mobile devices, wifi systems, medical equipment and other systems. The list of customers reads like a who's who of mobile device-makers: Apple, HTC, Motorola, Samsung and Nokia.

Based in Woburn, Skyworks has about 3,400 employees around the world and revenue for fiscal 2015 of $3.26 billion.

Teradyne Inc. is another longtime player in the semiconductor industry (and it, too, was founded by two MIT alums, Alex d'Arbeloff and Nick DeWolf), only its business model addresses one of the problems with making the chips: The manufacturing process is extremely complicated. As a result, testing new chips to make sure they work properly is important. Teradyne makes equipment used by the semiconductor manufacturers to test chips that came off production lines, and it also tests wireless equipment as well. Its customers include Intel, Samsung and Analog Devices. Teradyne had revenue of $1.6 billion in 2015. Headquartered in North Reading, Mass., it has about 3,900 employees.

Akamai — speeding up the Internet

Akamai Technologies was launched as a company in 1998 by mathematicians and scientists from the Massachusetts Institute of Technology and is based on the premise that smart application of mathematical algorithms would allow faster delivery of Internet content. Akamai has a vast array of customers, from the National Basketball Association to Airbnb. The increase in streaming video increased the need for Akamai's services, and the company also has branched into Internet security.

The company had fiscal 2015 revenue of $2.2 billion and has more than 6,200 employees around the world. Thomas Leighton, the CEO of Akamai, is a classic Boston-area tech story. As a mathematics professor at MIT, he worked on the algorithms that established the company in 1998.

The creation and growth of Akamai is a classic Boston-area tech success story.

The ground floor of Akamai's headquarters in Cambridge's Kendall Square looks like mission control for a space shuttle flight, which is in a way poetic given that the area was being prepared to house NASA in the early 1960s before the assassination of President John F. Kennedy. NASA would end up growing in Texas, the home state of President Lyndon B. Johnson, who took office after Kennedy's death.

Nuance Communications and the future of voice recognition

Nuance Communications, based in Burlington, Mass., was built largely around the notion that people would rather talk to their computers than type on keyboards. Many customers know the company through its Dragon line of products for computers and mobile devices like Apple's iPhone. Nuance is provides the technology for the Siri voice recognition system.

Voice recognition powered by companies such as Nuance is becoming increasingly popular as a way of authenticating a computer or device user's identity. Nuance, which also produces specialized products for industries such as health care, has more than 6,000 employees around the world. Nuance, which was founded in 1992, reported fiscal 2014 revenue of $1.9 billion. In addition to voice recognition, Nuance also has a significant imaging business.

Other billion-dollar Boston companies

American Tower isn't a pure technology company in the classic sense of the term. In many ways, it's a real estate operation. But technology is at the core of the business, which spun off as its own company in 1998. The Boston-based operation owns and operates mobile phone towers — about 144,000 sites around the world — and leases out access to mobile carriers. American Tower, which is based in Boston, also operates networks for some of its customers. American Tower took in over $4.8 billion in revenue in 2015.

PTC, formerly Parametric Technology Corporation, makes a variety of software for computer-aided product design and product lifecycle management.

The company, which employs about 6,000, also has a product that helps companies build Internet of Things applications. Revenue for 2015 was $1.25 billion. The company is based in Needham.

TripAdvisor, also based in Needham, has expanded rapidly since going public in 2011. The company provides reviews of travel-related content, combining the insight from other customers with the ability to quickly book a trip. TripAdvisor was founded in 2000 above a pizza shop in Needham – it just completed a new headquarters totaling 282,000 square feet. It has 3,400 full-time employees and 2015 revenue of $1.49 billion.

Wayfair is another fast-growing ecommerce company that went public in late 2014. Specializing in home goods, it has quickly surged over $2 billion in sales and 3,800 employees, many of them located in its Back Bay headquarters. Two business partners, Steve Conine and Niraj Shah, started the company in 2002 by selling media stands and storage furniture.

Clean Harbors is well known as being a first responder for the environment. The company often is called to mitigate the environmental impact of industrial or shipping accidents. As important as its disaster-response business is, Clean Harbors derives much of its revenue from long-term engagements to help industrial companies deal with environmentally sensitive materials. A subsidiary specializes in the disposal of used motor oil. Clean Harbors was founded in 1980 by a Northeastern graduate, Alan McKim, and is headquartered in Norwell, south of Boston. The company has approximately 12,900 employees. Revenue for the 2015 fiscal year was a little more than $3.27 billion.

Large out-of-state tech presence

Many of the nation's largest tech companies have a sizable presence in the Boston area.

IBM runs what it says is its largest software development laboratory in North America in Littleton. The campus has more than 3,400 software experts, according to the company. Between its other sites in Massachusetts, including Waltham and Cambridge, IBM is believed to employ about 5,000 in the state, and with the growth of its IBM Watson division, headquartered in Cambridge, it continues to expand here.

Cisco Systems, one of the world's largest tech employers, has about 1,500 employees in Massachusetts, most of them at its Boxborough, Mass. facility. Like IBM, it became a major player in Massachusetts largely through a series of acquisitions.

Google has a significant operation in Cambridge and did much of the work building its Android mobile device operating system here. It has about 970 employees at its Cambridge site, driven largely by its acquisition of ITA Software in 2012.

Microsoft also has a substantial Massachusetts operation in the heart of Kendall Square. An estimated 900 people work there in an assortment of disciplines, and it's near another Microsoft facility, its New England Research and Development Center.

Facebook has been growing its presence in Cambridge with an engineering center focused on data storage, security, and networking. About 100 employees work at its Kendall Square site.

Amazon has made significant inroads as a Massachusetts employers the past few years, first by acquiring warehouse robot maker Kiva Systems in 2012 and then establishing a Cambridge R&D center. In July 2016 Amazon opened a new warehouse in Fall River and was looking to fill 500 positions.

Up-and-coming public companies

Pegasystems, a fast-growing Cambridge company that creates software to automate complex business processes. Pegasystems founder and CEO Alan Trefler is a chess master and an outspoken leader on the future of tech in Boston.

Endurance International, based in Burlington, Mass., provides web-building tools and web hosting services, competing with the likes of Go Daddy and Web.com. Endurance is based in Burlington and has 2,500 employees. Endurance recently acquired a well-known local public company, Constant Contact, an online marketing company that provides tools for email newsletters and other online communications.

LogMeIn provides cloud-based services for individuals and businesses for facilitating file and screen collaboration and also has an Internet of Things product that allow users to monitor and control equipment remotely. The company is headquartered in a recently renovated warehouse in South Boston.

HubSpot is an in-bound marketing company providing software to businesses to help them expand their exposure and grow their businesses using a variety of web-based methods. The company, based in Cambridge, went public in October 2014 and has about 1,500 employees.

iRobot is the Boston area's most successful robotics company, known for its Roomba vacuuming robot, along with new products the mop and scrub floors. The company is based in Bedford, Mass., and has about 500 employees. Colin Angle is the CEO and co-founder.

EnerNOC is a cleantech company that makes software that enables big energy users to get paid for reducing their consumption. It also provides energy intelligence software, helping companies optimize energy efficiency, procurement and risk management. Based in South Boston, EnerNOC has about 800 employees.

Boston's world-leading position in health care

Boston is a national health care powerhouse, the home to some of the highest-rated hospitals in the world and an incubator for research to cure diseases. Health care in Boston helps form the bedrock for the region's economy. It's an ongoing source of job growth and spawns innovations that often lead to dynamic companies.

Our world-class health care system also is expensive and under considerable pressure to rein in costs. It is approaching a period of change that will challenge conventional approaches to delivering care with new technologies and non-traditional locations.

Even if you aren't a medical professional, there are many job opportunities in local health care.

The scope of Greater Boston's health care industry is enormous. About 167,000 people work in hospitals and other health care settings in Greater Boston, according to the Bureau of Labor Statistics. About 10,000 are doctors or surgeons, the latter earning an average of about $220,000 per year. Some 44,000 in the region are registered nurses. Boston has about 25 percent more registered nurses than the national average, and the average salary was about $95,000 in 2015, according to federal data.

Even if you aren't a medical professional, there are many job opportunities in the Boston area health care ecosystem. The diversity of occupations is exemplified by Massachusetts General Hospital (MGH), Boston's largest hospital, which billed over $3.46 billion in net revenue in 2015. MGH, like most other Boston hospitals, has needs in finance, administration, information technology, human resources and facilities management, among other areas.

Boston's health care and social assistance industry employs over 130,000 people in the city alone, or nearly 19 percent of the jobs located within the city, according to a recent report by the Boston Planning and Development Authority.

Boston is a magnet for the best medical talent and for patients seeking the best medical care. Aside from Mass. General, the city's top health care institutions include Brigham and Women's Hospital, Boston Children's Hospital, Beth Israel Deaconness, and Boston Medical Center, Tufts Medical Center, and the Dana Farber Cancer Institute.

Here are the **employee numbers, in terms of full-time equivalents, at the Boston area's largest hospitals**, as of November 2015, according to the Boston Business Journal:

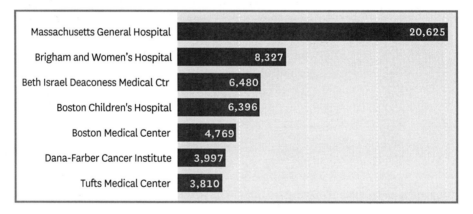

Hospital	FTEs
Massachusetts General Hospital	20,625
Brigham and Women's Hospital	8,327
Beth Israel Deaconess Medical Ctr	6,480
Boston Children's Hospital	6,396
Boston Medical Center	4,769
Dana-Farber Cancer Institute	3,997
Tufts Medical Center	3,810

It's an open question whether the Boston area's hospitals will collectively grow jobs over the next few years, even as the economy continues to improve. The reason: an ever-growing concern about costs, and the new regulations that have been created, both on the state and federal level, to try to contain them. It is clear that the kind of jobs the health care system is creating will continue to evolve as the emphasis on technology to reduce costs continues to grow. And as regulations become more complex, there will be demand for people who can help health care institutions navigate them.

With six major teaching hospitals, Boston is in its own league as a medical hub. But even Boston's top health care institutions are being challenged to change, said Andrew Dreyfus, the CEO of Blue Cross Blue Shield of Massachusetts. Hospitals will remain under pressure to transition from the inpatient, hospital center model to the outpatient, community center model. And it's not just for costs, but because patients are going to demand it. "If you think about businesses that have oriented themselves around customer needs, health care may be one of the last sectors of the economy that hasn't done that. In some ways today's hospitals are still oriented toward the needs of the professionals who work in the hospital, so whether it's when are surgeries scheduled, how seamless and coordinated is the care, you still have to go from place to place to place," Dreyfus said.

But a more customer-centric evolution will emerge, Dreyfus said. "In the future people are going to demand and want and need much more coordinated care, first of all for their health and secondly it's what a reasonable expectation is for consumers. … Certainly my children's generation is not going to be calling people up on the phone to make appointments or get information or data or to select when they're going to get their care as my generation did. And people are going to increasingly rely on wearable devices, even ingestible devices."

Medical research

Boston parlayed its academic reputation and early success as a center for medical innovation to become the health care leader it is today. Boston's health care innovations date back as far back as 1846, when the first public demonstration of a surgery using an anesthetic was performed in what is now known at the Ether Dome at Mass. General Hospital. But firsts came from many other hospitals as well, including the first success cardiac surgery (Boston Children's Hospital in 1938); the first successful organ transplant (Brigham and Women's Hospital in 1954).

Boston's prowess in medical research has been rewarded with a disproportionate amount of funding from the National Institutes of Health, the federal agency that underwrites some $30 billion annually in biomedical research.

In fiscal year 2015, Massachusetts' constellation of research hospitals, concentrated in Boston, received $2.5 billion in NIH funding, 10 percent of NIH research funding, second only to California, but easily the most funding per capita in the nation. Here are the **top five recipients of NIH funding in Massachusetts:**

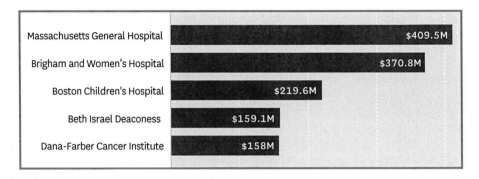

Massachusetts General Hospital	$409.5M
Brigham and Women's Hospital	$370.8M
Boston Children's Hospital	$219.6M
Beth Israel Deaconess	$159.1M
Dana-Farber Cancer Institute	$158M

Partners HealthCare — and its independent competition

Boston has one dominant health care provider: Partners HealthCare, a group of hospitals and physician groups that include Mass. General, Brigham and Women's, Spaulding Rehabilitation Hospital, and several suburban Boston hospitals, including North Shore Medical Center and Newton-Wellesley Hospital. Partners employs over 60,000. Because of its clout in setting health care costs, it has come under political pressure as it continues to expand. Massachusetts' health care costs are among the highest in the country, stoking concern that the state's success as a health care leader is coming at the cost of high health care premiums, and ultimately, job creation in the state.

Partners has plenty of competition from independent hospitals in Boston alone, such as Beth Israel Deaconess Medical Center, Boston Medical Center, and Tufts Medical Center.

Steward Health Care

Steward Health Care is a sizable exception in the Massachusetts hospital environment. It's a for-profit enterprise, founded by the purchase of a nonprofit group of hospitals — Caritas Christi — in 2010 by the private equity group Cerberus Capital Management. With additional acquisitions, Steward today has nine hospitals and 17,000 employees. Although Steward is a for-profit, it came into the Boston area market believing it could charge less than many of the Boston-area nonprofit hospitals and still make a profit.

After years of losses, Steward reported in early 2015 that all but one of its hospitals is profitable.

Health insurers

The Boston area's health insurance companies are regularly rated among the best in the country. The three top locally based firms are: Blue Cross Blue Shield of Massachusetts, Harvard Pilgrim Health Care, and Tufts Health Plan.

Unlike some of the large national insurers such as Aetna and Cigna, the Boston insurance leaders are nonprofits. Like health care providers, the health insurers are under pressure to control costs and create new products while also adapting to new regulations. All the same, the health insurers, like the hospitals, are large enterprises with a wide assortment of job opportunities. A quick glance at Blue Cross Blue Shield's job listings underscores the need for talent: There are job postings for data analysts, sales personnel, communications specialists, and recruiters.

Electronic medical records companies, digital health

The potential for information technology to help deliver services in health care has spawned companies around the country. The Boston area sees itself as a leader in digital health as the convergence of new technology and traditional health care continues. Many local companies have emerged, and below are four among many that have experienced rapid growth:

Athenahealth provides software to health care providers for an array of services, including simplifying the insurance billing process. In essence, athenahealth's software makes it easier to collect reimbursement from insurers, providing a greater monetary yield and fewer headaches. This innovation, among others, catapulted athenahealth from the startup phase to a successful public company with 4,600 employees and over $925 million in 2015 revenue. The company is based in Watertown, Mass.

eClinicalWorks has grown rapidly in the electronics medical records space, providing computerized records to health care providers and tools to help medical professionals communicate with their patients. The company introduced a mobile app in 2013 that allows patients to access their health records. EClinicalWorks has a cloud-based IT system that hosts approximately one-fifth of the nation's medical records. Based in Westborough, Mass., the company has 4,000 employees, and announced in the fall of 2015 it would add another 1,000 local jobs as it expands into a building formerly owned by EMC.

American Well is an innovator in the telehealth space, connecting patients to medical professionals through online connections. The company, based in downtown Boston, has raised over $120 million on the premise that telehealth will revolutionize the way patients receive care.

IBM Watson Health launched in 2015 and picked Cambridge as its headquarters, where at least 700 employees are expected to work. IBM Watson is a highly sophisticated and ambitious digital health effort: Its mission is to deploy the supercomputer Watson to analyze health care data to deliver more efficient and effective care. As artificial intelligence becomes more prominent in health care, IBM chose the health care capital of the U.S. to build out its new venture.

Some people to know in health care:

Andrew Dreyfus

Andrew Dreyfus is the CEO of Blue Cross Blue Shield of Massachusetts and widely known as thought leader in health care trends and affordability.

Ralph de la Torre is the CEO of Steward Health Care, the group of for-profit hospitals that is owned by private equity firm Cerberus.

Kate Walsh is the CEO of Boston Medical Center, home to the largest 24-hour trauma center in New England.

David Torchiana is the CEO of Partners HealthCare, the state's largest group of hospitals, including Massachusetts General and Brigham and Women's.

Sandy Fenwick is the CEO of Boston Children's Hospital, considered one of the best children's hospitals in the country.

Jonathan Bush is the outspoken CEO of athenahealth and author of Where Does It Hurt?: An Entrepreneur's Guide to Fixing Health Care.

Atul Gawande is a surgeon at Brigham and Women's Hospital, a public health researcher and the author of four books on health care, including Being Mortal: Medicine and What Matters in the End.

Dr. James O'Connell is the founding physician and president of Boston Health Care for the Homeless, a program that evolved to include to a 104-bed medical center for the homeless.

Lynn Nicholas is the president and CEO of the Massachusetts Hospital Association, the trade association for the state's 79 hospitals.

Boston: the nation's biotech capital

The biotechnology industry is all about fulfilling the most fundamental of human needs: To help people live longer, healthier lives. To that end, the Boston area has played a larger role than anywhere else in the world, producing drugs that have turned some deadly cancers into chronic, but manageable diseases, or allowing those with rare disorders that were once considered a death sentence to live for years beyond their previously expected lifespan.

The Boston area has for many years had one of the world's most vibrant life sciences clusters on the planet. A decade ago, Boston was considered by many to be in a dead heat with the San Francisco area for the world's largest biotech cluster, but today Massachusetts is the undisputed winner. In just the past few years, an increasing number of big pharmaceutical firms have opened or expanded in the area. In particular, Shire Pharmaceuticals has grown quickly over the past couple years to become one of the largest in the state, employing more than 3,000 people here in field of not only research, but sales, administration and regulatory compliance. That influx of new is likely one of the reasons that the 2015 annual ranking by the Genetic Engineering and Biotechnology News has ranked the state as the No. 1 biotech cluster in the nation in 2015 and 2016 (San Francisco is second).

The Boston area is the place life sciences companies, especially their R&D departments, feel they need to be, close to the brightest people and the most innovative ideas. Thus, a critical mass of leading biotech and pharma companies and world-class universities and hospitals has made the region a magnet for both domestic and international companies. The Massachusetts Institute of Technology and Harvard Medical School have both churned out some of the best scientists in the world to lead the research efforts in local biotech firms. Researchers such as MIT professor Robert Langer and Harvard geneticist George Church have together helped found dozens of companies. Massachusetts General Hospital, Dana-Farber Cancer Institute and Brigham and Women's Hospital are among the top hospitals in the country to conduct new drug trials.

The biggest local life sciences players

Here are the biggest and most-watched local companies in the pharmaceutical space:

Biogen: The state's largest independently owned biotech firm, Biogen was founded in 1978 and moved to Cambridge in 1982. The company has more than 7,000 employees worldwide, and made a name for itself with drugs for multiple sclerosis, starting with the approval of Avonex in 1996. In 2013 the company launched Tecfidera, a pill for the treatment of MS that quickly became the world's most prescribed drug for the disease. In 2015 the company made $10.8 billion in revenue, and it has been the state's most valuable biotech (in terms of market capitalization) for the past several years, more valuable than companies in other sectors with many times more employees. It is based in Cambridge's Kendall Square.

Vertex Pharmaceuticals: The state's second-largest, locally owned biotech was founded in the late 1980s by a group of venture capitalists and scientists

but was led in the early days by Josh Boger, who was CEO until 2009. The company's first drug was Incivek, an interferon-based treatment for hepatitis C approved in 2011 but which only lasted a couple of years before being overtaken by interferon-free drugs like Sovaldi. It currently has two approved drugs, the first ever to slow the progression of cystic fibrosis for some patients. Orkambi, approved in July 2015, promises to generate $5 billion in revenue within a couple of years, potentially making the company profitable for years to come.

Vertex Pharmaceuticals

Sanofi Genzyme: Founded in 1981 (under the name Genzyme) with a focus on drugs for very rare diseases of a type called lysosomal storage diseases. Its first drug was approved in the 1980s to treat Gaucher disease, and today it sells at least 10 treatments — many for rare diseases like Fabry and Pompe, in addition to Aubagio and Lemtrada for multiple sclerosis. The company was acquired by French pharma giant Sanofi in 2011.

The Broad Institute: Founded in 2003 as a joint research project between Harvard and MIT aimed at creating new approaches to disease, the nonprofit organization combines laboratories, programs and platforms, and scientists work to tackle critical problems in human biology and disease. The institute's facility at 320 Charles Street in Cambridge contains one of the largest genome sequencing centers in the world.

Shire Pharmaceuticals: Although technically based in Ireland, Shire's U.S. headquarters and most of its executives are in Lexington. The company began in 1986 with treatments for osteoporosis, then moved on to drugs for ADHD and rare diseases. Today the company has more than 22,000 employees world-wide since its 2016 acquisition of Baxalta, and has been building up its presence in Massachusetts for the past few years.

The biotech business model: high risks and rewards

Because biotechnology often deals with not just profits and revenues, but complex biology and chemistry, it's different from other industries. But essentially biotech companies are developing products to treat disease, and investors place bets on those companies whose products are most likely to be in demand by consumers. Demand for a new drug is a function of not only how effective it is at fighting disease, but how convenient it is to administer, how easy it is to transport and how many competing drugs there are for that same disease.

One unique aspect of biotech companies is that they can exist for years, even decades, without ever generating revenue from the sale of a single product. That's because the development of a new drug is a long, expensive process. According to a 2014 study by the Tufts Center for the Study of Drug Development, it costs $2.6 billion to develop a single new drug, factoring in the loss of more immediate profits the money used for research and development would have made. That's up from about $1 billion in 2003, adjusted for inflation. The study also found that the average time from synthesis of a drug to approval is 10.7 years, and only one out of eight drugs that makes it to human trials ever makes it to market.

But if a drug ultimately wins regulatory approval, the resulting revenue usually more than compensates for the upfront costs. The high prices drugmakers are able to charge, especially in the U.S., has been a topic of much debate in recent years, brought to the forefront by the "$1,000-a-pill" drug for hepatitis C, Sovaldi, launched in 2014 by Gilead Sciences. Those high costs are often defended by drug companies as needed to recover the costs that went into the product's development and to provide an incentive for investors to buy shares.

Biotech's impact on other industries

The growth of biotech in the past several years has spilled over into other supporting industries. Large contract research organizations, such as Parexel and Charles River Labs, have grown into major global employers by serving the many small and "virtual" biotech companies that have been formed.

But outside of research-related companies, the industry has also spurred growth in several other areas, such as construction. The state added 5.1 million square feet of lab space from 2007 to 2014, with a total inventory of 21.2 million square feet as of 2014, according to MassBio. Financial firms, consulting firms and public relations firms have all found fertile ground to grow in the area by catering to the biotech industry.

Despite the attention Sovaldi received, with an annual, per-patient cost of $94,000 when launched, it is far from the most expensive drug. Treatments for rare diseases can command annual costs of as much as $500,000, while the cost of new gene therapies expected to be approved in coming years is expected to be more than $1 million for a single treatment. Costs of new drugs are determined by how many patients are likely to take it, how effective it is and how long those patients will generally be on it.

Here are some blockbusters

Massachusetts biotech firms have developed their fair share of blockbuster drugs (defined in the industry as having sales of more than $1 billion annually). Following is a list of current and likely future blockbuster drugs already developed or in the works at companies in the state.

Biogen: **Tecfidera** (for multiple sclerosis), launched in 2013: 2014 revenue of $3.6 billion; and **Avonex** (also for multiple sclerosis), launched in 1996: 2014 revenue of $3.0 billion.

EMD Serono in Rockland (the U.S. headquarters of the pharmaceutical arm of German firm, Merck KGaA): **Rebif** (for multiple sclerosis): 2015 revenue of $2.0 billion.

Takeda Oncology (formerly called Millennium Pharmaceuticals): **Velcade** (for multiple myeloma), launched in 2003: 2014 revenue of $2.9 billion.

Sanofi Genzyme: **Avonex**, for multiple sclerosis. With 2015 revenues of $863 million, it has not quite reached blockbuster status yet, but appears well on its way.

Vertex Pharmaceuticals, Boston: **Orkambi** (for cystic fibrosis), launched in July 2015. Analysts estimate that by 2018 it will have annual revenue of about $5 billion.

The science of drugs

There were 1,645 drugs in clinical development (human tests) in the state in 2015, about 13 percent of the total in the U.S., according to MassBio, the local life sciences trade group. Cancer drugs make up the biggest part of that pipe-line, about 36 percent, with anti-infectives and diseases of the central nervous system are the second- and third-largest, respectively, making up 15 percent and 14 percent of the total drugs being developed.

Most drugs are divided into two categories: small-molecule drugs, which are almost always in pill form; and large-molecule, or biologics, which are administered intravenously or injected. While small molecules are much cheaper to manufacture than biologics, there are limits as to what can be done with them. Drugs made through biological (rather than purely chemical) processes are becoming more popular, with about 40 percent of new drugs in development in the Boston area now being biologics.

The creation of a biologic drug is far more complex and costly, but they have the advantage (for drug companies) that it is much harder for competitors to make generic copies; the competition for such drugs often is limited even after the patents expire on them.

One recent trend has been toward drugs that target a specific genetic profile, called targeted therapies. In early 2015, President Barack Obama proposed a Precision Medicine Initiative to fuel research into the genetic markers underlying many diseases, and the development of therapies to treat them. Such drugs can either block (inhibitors) or spur the production of (agonists) certain proteins involved in disease by affecting the way the genes work.

Another emerging trend is drug and device combinations, such as drug-elut-ing stents, or a matchstick-sized device by Boston-based Intarcia for type

> Another fast-emerging technology is gene therapy, which involves actually replacing disease-causing DNA with healthy or "corrected" versions.

2 diabetes that would be inserted into the abdomen to deliver a steady dose of a drug over the course of an entire year.

Yet another fast-emerging technology is gene therapy, which involves actually inserting healthy DNA into a patient who has a mutation. Locally, Cambridge-based bluebird bio, Genzyme and Voyager Therapeutics are all working on such therapies. A related, newer field is gene editing, where a patient's own mutations are actually cut out and replaced, and companies like Editas Medicine and Intellia Therapeutics are leading such research. While such treatments are likely to be very expensive when they are eventually approved, they are cures rather than ongoing treatments for disease, potentially saving money in the long run.

The latest science would not be possible without the sequencing of the human genome through most of the 1990s and early 2003, a process that was greatly helped by local researchers. It was that act of identifying the chemical base pairs that make up human DNA that has made possible an explosion of new approaches to how drugs can affect the human body. Two decades earlier, Walter Gilbert and Allan Maxam developed a method of sequencing at a laboratory at Harvard, and the Whitehead Institute in Cambridge was one of the main centers for the Human Genome Project.

IPO frenzy

After a long dry spell since even before the economic crash of 2008, the appetite among investors for biotech shares has grown exponentially (although, toward the middle of 2015, biotech stocks went through a rough stretch). More than 30 biotech companies in Massachusetts alone went public from March 2013 through June 2015, raising well over $2 billion. Many of those companies had just a handful of employees; one, in fact, had just two for its IPO. Following is a list of the 10 Massachusetts-based companies that held the biggest IPOs since the current boom began in March 2013.

Intellia Therapeutics (Nasdaq: NTLA), Cambridge. May 2016. $163 million. Gene editing.

Blueprint Medicines (Nasdaq: BPMC), Cambridge. April 2015. $147 million. Cancer drugs.

Seres Therapeutics (Nasdaq: MCBM), Cambridge. June 2015. $133 million. Drugs that target the microbiome.

Akebia Therapeutics (Nasdaq: AKBA), Cambridge. March 2014. $115 million. Drugs for chronic kidney disease and cancers.

Karyopharm Therapeutics (Nasdaq: KPTI), Newton. November 2013. $108 million. Cancer drugs

Agios Pharmaceuticals (Nasdaq: AGIO), Cambridge. July 2013. $106 million. Cancer drugs.

Sage Therapeutics (Nasdaq: SAGE), Cambridge. July 2014. $104 million. Drugs for diseases of the central nervous system.

bluebird bio (Nasdaq: BLUE), Cambridge. June 2013. $101 million. Gene therapy for blood disorders.

Tokai Pharmaceuticals (Nasdaq: TKAI), Cambridge. September 2014. $98 million. Cancer drugs.

Zafgen (Nasdaq: ZFGN), Boston. June 2014. $96 million. A drug to fight obesity.

Jobs in the industry

The number of jobs created by the biotech industry and how much it has grown in recent years has been a matter of some debate within the state. That's largely because when former Gov. Deval Patrick launched the $1 billion, 10-year Life Science Initiative in 2007, he said it would create 250,000 new jobs. As of 2015, it has created nowhere near that number, even factoring in his comment during the same speech to the effect that every life science job creates three to four others in other fields. According to the 2016 MassBio Industry Snapshot, there were about 63,000 jobs in the biopharma sector as of 2014, an increase of 37 percent from a decade earlier.

Salaries specifically in the drugs and pharmaceutical industries average $107,000.

The kinds of jobs the sector creates generally pay well. Jobs in biotech in Massachusetts earned an average annual salary of $147,000 in 2015, significantly higher than average and contributing $9.3 billion to the total state's payroll.

There are 18 job categories under the federal Bureau of Labor Statistics that are considered "life sciences," which encompasses medical devices as well as pharmaceuticals. In Massachusetts, the largest single category by far is in biotech research and development, which accounted for 31,469 jobs in 2015.

One area of biotechnology that's seeing growing demand is big data specialists to analyze the huge amounts of information generated by drug and medical device trials. With one goal of the industry to find ways to shorten the development time for new drugs and reduce the size of trials, more and more data is being collected during the course of trials to show how a drug works. Beyond trials, enormous effort is being put into combing through the 3 billion base pairs of DNA to find genetic markers for diseases that can become the targets of new drugs. Analyzing such huge amounts of data requires specialists in the art of informatics and data analysis.

Some people to know in the industry

Here are some of the leaders in the local biotech industry:

David Meeker, executive vice president and head of Sanofi Genzyme: As head of the state's biggest biotech employer, Meeker wields considerable influence. More than any other local company, Sanofi Genzyme has helped create the Massachusetts biotech ecosystem through former executives who have gone on to found or work for other biotechs, and Meeker knows a considerable number of them.

Deborah Dunsire: Best known as CEO of Millennium Pharmaceuticals for eight years until 2013, Dunsire oversaw that company's acquisition by Japanese big pharma company Takeda in 2008. After she left that role she was named CEO of Forum Pharmaceuticals, which attempted to develop a drug to treat Alzheimer's which ultimately failed. Dunsire has been a mentor to dozens of local women in biotech.

Jeffrey Leiden: The chairman, president and CEO of Vertex Pharmaceuticals joined Vertex as CEO in 2011. He has presided over the introduction of the ground-breaking cystic fibrosis drug Orkambi while also moving the company to gleaming new headquarters on the Boston waterfront.

Bob Coughlin *(Bill Brett photo)*

Bob Coughlin, CEO of MassBio: A former state representative, Coughlin has headed the state's industry organization since 2007. The organization counts more than 700 companies as members, and with the number of life sciences companies in the state exploding, membership is growing quickly.

Bob Langer, MIT chemical engineering professor: Langer joined the faculty of MIT in 1974, and in 2005 was named an "institute professor," the highest honor awarded by the university to faculty. He also has well over 1,000 patents, many of which have been licensed to drug, chemical, biotech and medical device companies. He has helped found more than two dozen companies, including Momenta Pharmaceuticals, InVivo Therapeutics and Bind Therapeutics. His innovations are estimated to have helped some 2 billion cancer patients around the world.

George Church, professor of Genetics at Harvard Medical School: His innovations have been used in genome sequencing methods since the mid-1990s. He has co-founded several area companies, among them Knome, Joule, Gen9, Editas and Warp Drive Bio.

Michelle Dipp, former CEO of OvaScience: Educated as a doctor at Oxford University, Dipp became an executive at Sirtis Pharmaceuticals while still in her 20s, co-founded the venture capital firm Longwood Fund. Dipp is considered among the most well-connected and influential biotech leaders in the area. She remains executive chairwoman at OvaScience, which develops treatments for infertility.

John Maraganore, CEO of Alnylam Pharmaceuticals: As both head of one of the area's largest biotech firms (its first drug is hoped to reach market sometime in 2018) and as a board member of the national organization, BIO, Maraganore has been a vocal defender of the industry in the face of recent drug price controversy. Maraganore was an executive at Biogen until he became the founding CEO at Alnylam in 2002.

Henri Termeer: Best known as CEO of Genzyme Corp. for more than 30 years until its acquisition by Sanofi in 2011, Termeer was largely responsible for building the company into the rare disease drug giant it is today. He now serves in chairman and advisory roles in several area biotech firms.

Noubar Afeyan, Flagship founder and CEO: The son of survivors of the Armenian genocide, Afeyan started one of the area's foremost venture capital firms devoted to investing in and creating new life science firms in 2001. Flagship has $1.4 billion under management, and in 2015 it raised the largest of the funds raised by four area VC firms for life sciences. Some of Flagship's successes have included Acceleron Pharma and Tetraphase Pharmaceuticals.

Kevin Starr: The co-founder of Third Rock Ventures, which has raised $1.3 billion through three funds. Starr functions as CEO through the first year to 18 months after launch, having led companies including Agios Pharmaceuticals, SAGE Therapeutics and Zafgen. He was formerly COO and CFO of Millennium Pharmaceuticals.

Tony Coles: Originally from the Boston area, where he was an executive at Vertex Pharmaceuticals, Coles moved away in 2006 and eventually landed at Onyx Pharmaceuticals in South San Francisco in early 2009, and headed the company until its $9.7 billion acquisition by Amgen. In 2014 he returned to the area to head Yumanity, a biotech focused on Alzheimer's and other diseases. He is one of just a handful of African-American biotech executives worldwide.

Boston's medical device leaders: The mechanical side of life sciences is booming

While the aim of the pharmaceutical industry is to create molecules that can affect the body's biological processes, the medical device industry tries to create physical devices to improve human health. There are many similarities between the two fields: Both are heavily regulated by the U.S. Food and Drug Administration, and both depend on scientific innovations and technological breakthroughs for new products. But since most medical devices don't take as long to bring to market as drugs do, and tend to have lower profit margins, companies that make them more closely resemble businesses outside the realm of life sciences.

Massachusetts has produced some of the world's biggest medical device companies: Boston Scientific was an early leader in stents and pacemakers; Alere is recognized as one of the top developers of diagnostic tests; and Thermo Fisher has dominated the scientific instruments market. While scientific instruments are not used directly in the care of patients, their central role in the research that produces new drugs and devices means they are generally classified along with medical devices, as there is a great deal of overlap in the clients and the ultimate aim of those instruments.

Medical device growth in Massachusetts

Publicly held medical device companies worldwide generated revenue of $342 billion in 2014, up 2 percent from the previous year, according to a recent report by accounting firm Ernst & Young. In the U.S., medical device firms account for about two-thirds of the industry's total revenues. The number of public companies grew 9 percent from the previous year to 414, while employment at those companies grew just 2 percent to 678,500.

The number of medical device companies in Massachusetts has more than doubled over the last two decades to 436 as of 2016, according to the state's lobbying group, MassMEDIC. The state also had more device approvals by the Food and Drug Administration in 2015 than any other year in the past decade. In the past five years, Bay State medtech IPOs raised $51 million.

According to the Medical Device and Diagnostic Industry Online, the fastest growing jobs in medical technology from 2012 to 2014 were those for electrical and electronic equipment mechanics, installers, and repairers. Other jobs expected to grow quickly are natural sciences managers; biological technicians; and electrical, electronics, and electromechanical assemblers.

Among the fastest-growing areas of medical devices in 2013 are companies developing diagnostic tests. That's largely due to the booming biotechnology and pharmaceutical sector, as drugmakers try and find new ways to increase the efficiency of their R&D efforts by targeting more and more specific populations of patients that are likely to respond favorably to their drugs.

Major companies in medical devices

Here are the top six companies headquartered in the state by 2014 revenue.

1. **Thermo Fisher Scientific.** HQ: Waltham. 2015 revenue: $17.0 billion. With 50,000 global employees, the company is one of the state's largest employers, although most of its employees don't work in the state. It makes medical and diagnostic devices and scientific and lab equipment.

2. **Boston Scientific.** HQ: Marlborough. 2015 revenue: $7.5 billion. The company was founded in 1979 and became one of the world's leading suppliers and developers of pacemakers and stents. It has branched out over the past decade into diagnostic devices for the heart, lungs and digestive system, as well as implantable devices to manage chronic neuropathic pain and neurological diseases.

3. **Alere.** HQ: Waltham. 2015 revenue: $2.5 billion. The company specializes in point-of-care diagnostic devices that give results quickly. In early 2016, Illinois-based Abbott Laboratories bid $5.8 to buy Alere, but the acquisition was stalled as of November 2016 after Alere disclosed errors in revenues and federal subpoenas of which Abbott said it was unaware.

4. **Hologic.** HQ: Bedford. 2015 revenue: $2.7 billion. With a focus on women's health, Hologic's main products are used for the detection and diagnosis of breast cancer. It also develops devices used in surgery and diagnostics.

5. **Waters Corp.** HQ: Milford. 2015 revenue: $2 billion. The company was founded in the mid-1990s with a focus on two specific technologies central to life science lab research: chromatography (the separation of chemicals) and mass spectrometry (analysis of chemicals).

6. **Bruker Corp.** HQ: Billerica. 2015 revenue: $1.6 billion. Founded in Germany in 1961 by Günther Laukien, the company is still one-third owned by the Laukien family and is now headed by his son, Frank Laukien, and makes a range of lab equipment ranging from magnetic resonance technology and mass spectrometry to imaging equipment used in preclinical drug trials.

Other key local medical device companies include Covidien, which in 2014 became a subsidiary of Medtronic for $42.9 billion; Phillips Healthcare, which employs 3,500 in Andover, Mass.; Smith & Nephew, also in Andover; PerkinElmer, which is the world leader in newborn testing diagnostics; ZOLL Medical, which focuses on resuscitation devices; and Haemonetics Corp., which focuses on blood-related products.

People to know in medical devices

Mike Mahoney: The CEO of Boston Scientific since 2013, Mahoney's tenure at the helm has coincided with a significant turnaround at the company. While opinions are mixed as to how much credit ought to go to him for the recent successes, there is general agreement that he re-energized the company and turned it from a company frequently focused on cleaning up after past mistakes to one that's forward-looking and focused again on new products.

Marc Casper: Casper joined one of the precursor companies to Thermo Fisher in 2001 and was named its CEO in 2008. With the $13.6 billion acquisition of Life Technologies in 2013, the company has become the state's biggest company by annual revenue.

Donald Ingber: the founding director of the Wyss Institute for Biologically Inspired Engineering at Harvard University, Ingber is the driving force behind one of that institute's recent novel developments, so-called "organs on chips" that mimic the workings of human organs for the purpose of testing new drugs.

Tom Sommer: The leader of the state's industry group, MassMEDIC, since it was founded in 1996, Sommer has led local efforts to repeal the medical device tax in recent years. He has overseen the group's growth from 200 when he began to more than 400 member companies today.

PART TWO

Finance, professional services, real estate and marketing

Financial services: the money managers, banks and custodians

Boston is one of the world's money management capitals, home to an assortment of mutual fund companies and wealth managers that compete on a global scale. When you add other segments, including insurance, custodian banks, and community and regional banks, the Massachusetts financial services industry is one of the leading employment sectors in the region.

Financial services accounts for 164,000 jobs in Massachusetts, a number that has slowly climbed back from the financial meltdown during the Great Recession of 2008-2009.

Here are some of the dominant local players in financial services at glance:

- **Fidelity Investments**, the mutual fund giant that employs about 5,100 in the state and boasts $5.428 trillion in total customer assets as of June 30, 2016.

- **State Street Corp.**, known as a custodian bank for the financial transactions it enables between institutions, employs about 12,902 in Massachusetts.

- **Bank of America**, one of the nation's largest banks, has significant operations in downtown Boston and a wide branch network in the state.

- **Liberty Mutual**, a leading insurance company (number 73 on the Fortune 500), calls Boston its home and employs 4,400 in the capital city and 50,000 worldwide.

- **John Hancock**, an insurer that has been a signature brand in Boston even after it was purchased by a Canadian financial services company Manulife in 2004.

The birth of the mutual fund — and the rise of Boston's financial services industry

When the topic of innovation and Massachusetts comes up, the focus invariably turns toward science and engineering — laboratories at the Massachusetts Institute of Technology and Harvard University and the work of technology luminaries such as Edwin Land and Kenneth Olsen. But a powerful argument can be made that the single most important innovation in the history of the modern Massachusetts economy took place on the other side of the Charles — in the Boston offices of a new company called Massachusetts Financial Services (MFS).

It was there on March 21, 1924, MFS launched the Massachusetts Investors Trust — an investment vehicle widely heralded as America's first mutual fund. The idea behind it seems simple in hindsight but it revolutionize investing: Rather than picking stocks on their own, investors small and large instead could pool their money by buying shares in funds that would be professionally managed. That first fund bought shares in businesses including insurance companies, a radiator manufacturer and oil companies.

New laws, including the creation of the IRA and 401(k), helped spur growth in the financial services industry.

Imitators quickly followed. Some of the individuals involved in the creation of the Massachusetts Investors Trust would form what would become today's Eaton Vance. Loomis Sayles was founded in 1926. The predecessor to today's Pioneer Investments followed in 1928. Putnam Investments was launched in 1937.

Fidelity Investments was founded in 1946 — a latecomer to the game by Boston standards — but the privately held concern owned by the Johnson family would grow to become one of the largest mutual companies in the world.

New laws helped spur the sector's growth. In 1974, federal legislation allowed the creation of the Individual Retirement Account, or IRA. Legislation allowing the 401(k) would follow in 1978. The combined effect of the new regulations was to give a huge boost to the mutual fund industry by offering individuals and families tax incentives to save for retirement and to make it easy to use mutual funds to do so.

For the first time in the last five years, the mutual fund industry fell between 2014 and 2015, from $15.88 to $15.65 trillion dollars. About 43 percent of U.S. households, or about 53.6 million, held shares in mutual funds in mid-2015.

The growth of mutual fund companies and companies serving the sector would help propel Boston from a sleepy northern industrial city in the 1950s into a global financial center by the 1980s.

No one embodied that success more than Peter Lynch, who ran Fidelity's flagship Magellan Fund throughout the 1980s. Lynch would become something of a rock star in the investing world. As Magellan soared, so did Fidelity. A story — perhaps apocryphal — made the rounds in the early 1990s that Fidelity Chairman Edward "Ned" Johnson walked into the office of then-Gov. Michael Dukakis and killed a proposal that would have hit financial services companies particularly hard. His strategy: mentioning the amount of unused office space the company owned in Texas.

While still a major player in the Massachusetts economy, the sailing has not been all smooth for the actively managed mutual fund sector nationally or in the state.

One factor hurting the industry in Boston, especially, has been the rise of the index fund.

Fund companies make money on actively managed mutual funds — those run by managers who move money among investments — by charging fees to investors. The system worked very nicely for fund companies for years. But the system had its critics, most noticeably an influential investor named John Bogle, founder of Vanguard Group. Bogle built his Pennsylvania-based company largely around the premise that over time, few if any managers could outsmart the market so effectively that the costs of paying a manager to trade stocks were outweighed by the returns. Bogle promoted what are called index funds — mutual funds that mimic an index such as the Standard & Poor's 500.

> While still a major player in the Massachusetts economy, the sailing has not been all smooth for the actively managed mutual fund sector.

In 1993, there were 69 index funds in the United States. By 2015, there were 406. A significant amount of that growth came at the expense of the traditional mutual fund companies. In 2010, Vanguard surpassed Fidelity to become the country's largest mutual fund company. Vanguard's family of mutual funds remains the largest in the country, with total assets under management pegged at about $3.6 trillion, compared to Fidelity's $2.06 trillion.

The largest employers in the city's mutual fund and investment management industry, according to December 2013 Boston Redevelopment Authority data, are:

- **Fidelity Investments**, with about 5,000 workers in the city as of September 2015.
- **Wellington Management**, with about 1,450 workers in the city and $998 billion in assets under management.
- **Eaton Vance**, with about 900 employees in the city. Assets under management were $336.4 billion as of Oct. 2016.
- **MFS**, with about 1,190 workers in the city. Assets under management as of Oct. 2016 were $425 billion.
- **Putnam Investments**, with about 1,700 workers in the city. Mutual fund assets under management was $151 billion as of October 2016.
- **Pioneer Investment Management** has $252 billion under management (Sept. 2016) and reports having 1,000 employees in Boston.

Meanwhile, the sector continues to draw and spawn new companies to Boston.

Natixis Global Asset Management, which is owned by a French parent but has its Americas and Asia operation run from Boston, had roughly $874.5 billion in assets under management as of June 30, 2016. and has added to its headcount here in recent years. The company sells products through a number of well-known affiliates, such as Boston-based Loomis Sayles.

Some of the top-performing mutual funds in Boston are run by GMO LLC. Founded in 1977, the relative new kid on the block has $91 billion in assets under management as of June 30, 2016. GMO's chief investment strategist, who was one of its co-founders, is a widely respected Englishman named Jeremy Grantham.

As for that original Massachusetts Investors Trust fund launched in 1924 with $50,000: It boasted assets of $5.8 billion as of September, 2016.

The Custodians

In the days when stocks were represented by paper certificates and investors tended to hold them directly instead of through fund companies, owning shares was relatively simple. Still, there was a place for companies that oversaw the transfer of shares and the money with which those shares were purchased. That role has increased dramatically with the spike in volumes of shares traded and the creation of new financial instruments such as exchange traded funds, or ETFs.

Serving as the link between investment companies, funds and exchanges have proven big business for two companies, especially, in Boston: State Street Corp., founded in 1792 in Boston, is a vital presence in the city with about 7,800 workers here, according to the Boston Redevelopment Authority. BNY Mellon has major operations in the city, though a much smaller headcount of about 1,980. Both companies have additional employees in the suburbs.

State Street consists of three major units: Global Services, Global Advisors and Global Markets.

At State Street Global Services, the major businesses are accounting, cash management, custody services and fund administration. Some customers hire State Street Global Services for relatively straightforward record-keeping.

State Street Global Advisors is more of a traditional asset management business. Assets under management were $2.30 trillion as of March 31, 2016. State Street Global Advisors differs from a company like Fidelity in that SSGA caters especially to institutional investors such as insurance companies, pension funds and non-profit institutions that operate endowments.

State Street Global Markets runs research and trading operations. Research essentially entails identifying and analyzing potential investment opportunities. Trading operations work on behalf of the bank or clients to try to find the best deals when the time comes to buy or sell assets such as stocks or bonds. When you see on television a room full of (usually) men sitting in long rows of work stations, talking on more than one phone at a time and staring at banks of screens flashing row after row of numbers, that usually is a trading desk.

Just a few blocks from State Street's corporate headquarters is the tower occupied by one of its chief rivals: Bank of New York Mellon.

BNY Mellon is much smaller in Boston than State Street, but still has extensive operations including investment management, wealth management, asset servicing and capital management in Boston. With thousands of employees in the city, jobs range from sales and client servicing to trading and research, according to its website job postings.

BNY Mellon's custody operation is slightly larger than State Street's, with the most recent figure pegged at $29.5 trillion in June 2016.

Independent investment advisers

The custody banks offer broad services to big clients that do huge volumes of business. But another class of investor, often with substantial sums of money to invest, needs service on an entirely different scale. They include wealthy individuals and families who often turn to independent investment advisers — chiefly for specialized investment guidance.

Many men and women who are turning ideas into successful companies know it's wise to have others manage their money.

With wealth that in some cases began accumulating before the Revolutionary War, established Boston-area families have shown considerable appetite for these services. Newly successful entrepreneurs form another class of client for investment advisers. Many men and women who are turning ideas into successful companies know it's something else altogether to pick investments — even if they have the time to do so.

A major difference between investment advisers and fund firms is that in many cases, the advisers will invest a small amount on behalf of their clients but will shift much of the money to third parties that actually put the funds to work. The advisers tend to make their money by charging their clients fees.

Some of the largest advisers in Massachusetts, according to a Boston Business Journal survey of companies in the industry, are:

- **Cambridge Associates LLC** ($156 billion under management as of June 1, 2015).

- **GW&K Investment Management** ($30.1 billion directed for clients, as of June 2016).

- **Breckenridge Capital Advisors** ($25.3 billion directed for clients, as of June 2016).

- **Baystate Financial** ($19.3 billion as of June 2016).

- **Westfield Capital Management Co. LP** ($13.5 billion as of June 2016).

- **Fiduciary Trust Co.** ($11.4 billion directed for clients, as of June 2016).

Some of these companies are significant local employers. Cambridge Associates reported having 506 Massachusetts employees, according to the Boston Business Journal in 2016; Baystate Financial said it has 523 Massachusetts personnel.

One of the most successful companies in the wealth advisory space is Affiliated Managers Group, which has built a large public company (2015 revenue of $2.44 billion). by taking equity stakes in boutique investment managers. The company is based on the North Shore in Beverly, Mass.

Traditional banks

For all the attention investment firms and fund companies get, banks still play a major role in the Massachusetts economy. And they're major employers. The sector has remained highly competitive despite a spate of mergers and acquisitions that saw the disappearance of many longtime banking names like Bank of Boston, Fleet Financial, and BayBank.

Bank of America, which acquired Fleet Financial in 2004, is the undisputed deposit leader in Massachusetts.

Four of the largest banking operations in the state are units of large out-of-state operations.

Bank of America, the successor to names like Bank of Boston, BayBank and Shawmut Bank, is run out of Charlotte, N.C. **Santander**, doing business locally as Sovereign Bank until recently, is owned by a Spanish parent. **Citizens Bank** recently went public in the process of shedding its longtime parent company, the Royal Bank of Scotland; and **TD Bank**'s parent is Canadian.

Bank of America, which acquired FleetBoston Financial in 2004 and thus purchased a large Massachusetts footprint, is the undisputed deposit leader in Massachusetts with a 27.3 percent market share — that's $64.4 billion in deposits. Citizens Bank is a distant second at $29.8 billion in deposits as of June 30, 2015.

While those large banks fight for market share, banks that still are based in Massachusetts, but were largely seen as small players just a few years ago, have stepped up their game and grown.

Eastern Bank, the state's largest locally owned bank, has total assets of nearly $10 billion as of Sept. 30, 2016 and more than 1,800 employees. Eastern, with roots on the North Shore of Boston, now is headquartered in Boston and over branches in Massachusetts and New Hampshire.

Other sizable regional banks: Rockland Trust has assets of $7.8 billion and about 1,100 employees, according to the company's website in December, 2016. Middlesex Savings Bank, based in Natick, has a little more than 500 employees and assets of about $4.4 billion.

Other banks with a significant footprint locally include Boston Private Bank & Trust, which focuses on wealth management and private banking; and Century Bank, which focuses on commercial banking, has assets of $4.1 billion as of April, 2016 and 27 branches in Massachusetts. Some regional banks with headquarters outside of Boston have made significant inroads in the market, among them Webster Bank, which made a deal to take over 14 of Citigroup's Boston area branches early in 2016.

In all, Massachusetts has more than 200 savings banks and credit unions. One reason for the abundance of small banks is that many of the state's banks were chartered in the 1800s in distinct communities. Eastern Bank, for instance, was chartered in 1818; Rockland Trust was chartered in 1907 and Middlesex Savings in 1859.

It's important to note, though, that Federal Reserve interest rate policies implemented to combat the Great Recession of 2008 squeezed the ability of small banks to make profits the way they traditionally have done so. Many experts expect considerable consolidation.

Private equity — and Bain Capital

No financial institution has been quite as politicized as Bain Capital, the Boston private equity firm. The basic business model of private equity is to buy companies considered undervalued or underperforming — often with a lot of borrowed money — and turn them around for sale. Former presidential candidate Mitt Romney, one of the founders of Bain Capital, was a very successful capitalist, helping build Bain Capital into a powerhouse. It now has $75 billion under management, according to its website in late 2016, and aside from investing in companies, also runs hedge funds and invests in startups.

Other top local private equity firms abound, and include TA Associates, Summit Partners, Audax Group and Thomas H. Lee Partners.

Innovation, technology and the future of financial services

Like any sector, financial services produces innovators. But there's a key difference. In the age of the Internet, many innovators have emerged from college or graduate school to launch companies that upend entire industries. Think Google and advertising. In the financial world, the innovators tend to be men and women who learn a business at one of the established players, then go off to launch their own firms that serve niche needs. Here is a sample of fast-growing financial services startups:

Quantopian is a crowd-sourced hedge fund, creating a platform for "quants" – those who use computer generated data to make investment decisions – to devise successful algorithms. The startup has raised $48.8 million as of November, 2016.

Kensho uses artificial intelligence to crunch data to anticipate market moves and answer traders' questions, creating a new level of stock market analytics. Fortune magazine called it "a Siri for Wall Street." Kensho has raised nearly $58 million as of December 2016.

Goji provides online car insurance comparison shopping with a technology that allows customers to quickly compare the rates of major carriers. It's raised nearly $90 million and planned to employ 350 by September of 2016.

As technology becomes ever more embedded in financial services, more startups are jumping into the financial technology space. According to a 2015 story in the Boston Globe, about 100 startups are creating products in the fin-tech area. Driving their efforts is the mining of data — as the startup Kensho illustrates — to access insights and improve processes for financial services. That is why there is a strong premium on data scientists at every major financial services company.

Mobility, technology and the threat to financial services

Looking forward, a number of factors threaten Boston's status as a hub in the financial services industry.

The biggest threat may come from the ability to move work just about anywhere. Transactions today often live in computers from inception to completion, never making their way to paper. Fidelity Investments has found substantial cost savings by moving work to Rhode Island, New Hampshire, North Carolina and Texas. There's little reason companies won't similarly move work not only to other states, but also to other countries.

There also have been big changes in the ownership of a number of the city's prominent firms. John Hancock Financial Services, one of the biggest employers in Boston with about 3,800 employees in the city, is owned by Canada's ManuLife Financial. MFS Investment Management is owned by Sun Life of Toronto, Canada. One would he hard-pressed to find a civic leader who would not lament the sale of a local company to an out-of-town owner.

Technology is also driving efficiencies in financial services — in banking and money management in particular. Do-it-yourself online banking is disrupt-ing traditional bricks and mortar banking, and in wealth management, the advent of robo-advisers, computers powered by algorithms that smartly guide investors, is changing how retail investors receive financial advice.

Abby Johnson

Some people to know in Boston financial services

Abby Johnson, the chairwoman and CEO of Fidelity Investments, is perhaps the most famous (and least interested in fame) executive in Boston financial services. She has taken the reins of leadership from her father Ned Johnson, who grew Fidelity into a mutual fund giant.

Jay Hooley, the CEO of State Street Corp., runs a massive international financial services empire that all the same has a large impact on Boston, both as an employer and contributor to many civic initiatives.

Robert Reynolds, the CEO of Putnam Investments, joined Putnam in 2008 from Fidelity Investments, and has been active in advocating for the city's financial services industry and retirement planning.

Bob Rivers is the new CEO of Eastern Bank, responsible for running the region's largest locally owned bank that recently started an innovation lab to explore new financial services technology.

Barry Sloane is the president and CEO of Century Bank and Trust, a publicly traded bank and also considered one of New England's largest family-run banks.

John Hailer, president and CEO of Natixis Global Wealth Management, manages one of the region's fastest-growing financial services firms, with 1,400 Boston employees out of over 20,000 worldwide. He plays a leadership role at the New England Council and the Boston Public Library.

Thomas Faust is the CEO of Eaton Vance, a publicly traded fund company with revenue over $1.4 billion in 2015. Faust is an advocate for active investment management, and the firm's NextShares are designed to lower the cost of actively managed funds.

Anne Finucane is the global chief strategy and marketing officer for Bank of America, overseeing the advertising and public policy positioning of the bank. Finucane also chairs the bank's charitable foundation.

David Long is CEO of Liberty Mutual, the locally based insurer with $39.4 billion in 2015 revenue. The company said it plans to hire between 25,000 and 35,000 employees over the next five years.

Gerry Sargent is one of Citizens Bank's top executives, leading its middle market business companywide and overseeing the bank's state presidents throughout its national footprint.

Boston's vast world of professional services

Lawyers, accountants, IT consultants, and headhunters: Boston's economic success has created a fertile ground for a wide range of professional services. Almost all businesses, even the smallest ones, need legal, accounting and technology assistance. They also need management consultants, human resources consultants, temporary placement agencies, web designers, and a host of other specialized professionals who manage projects and help solve problems for companies. A strong local economy has an equally healthy professional services sector, and Boston's is especially vibrant.

It's important to note that there are many jobs at law firms for non-lawyers and even more jobs at accounting firms for non-accountants. In particular, the so-called Big Four accounting firms — PwC (PricewaterhouseCoopers), Deloitte, Ernst & Young, and KPMG — hire many employees outside of their core accounting function. For example, Ernst & Young employs over 2,000 people in Massachusetts, according to the 2016 Boston Business Journal Book of Lists, and yet only 559 are CPAs. Many others there provide consulting in various industries or work in support functions. Likewise, the largest law firm in Boston, Ropes & Gray, employs over 1,100 in Massachusetts — and fewer than half, 504, are lawyers. The Boston area's leading professional services firms are substantial businesses — Ropes & Gray did almost $1.4 billion in revenue in 2015 — that require workers in many disciplines, including finance, sales, tech support, and human resources.

The Boston legal scene

Massachusetts has among the highest density of lawyers per capita in the country, coming in third behind the District of Columbia and New York. The high population of lawyers speaks to one central fact: In a large, diverse economy like Boston's, lawyers are critical in helping companies drive business forward. The Boston area certainly has plenty of lawyers who attend to personal needs, like writing wills, handling divorces, and closing a home purchase. Boston's legal heft, however, derives from business-to-business activity. Lawyers help obtain patents and protect intellectual property; they smooth the path for international expansion; they're in the middle of companies' efforts to buy competitors; they help navigate regulatory hurdles when real estate developers seek to build new projects; they make sure companies are in compliance with a raft of regulations, including in employment law. And when startups go public (making their shares available to be purchased by the public), it's essential to have a legal team to craft the documents required by federal regulators. There is plenty more that lawyers do to help companies, and it's safe to say that it's almost impossible to be in business at any level without legal help.

The top 10 law firms in Boston, as measured by the number of local attorneys, all have significant business-to-business practices — and most of them have national and international offices. Many of their names reflect generations of local business history, and some are the product of mergers with out-of-town firms.

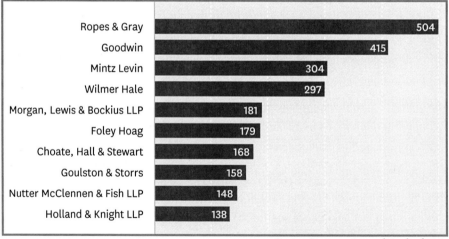

Boston Business Journal Book of Lists

While Boston has a fertile ecosystem for attorneys, local law firms are not immune to the economic trends weighing on the legal industry. Ever since the Great Recession and the near meltdown of the financial services industry (2008-2009), law firms have been under pressure to rein in their fees, and in turn, control their costs. The number of attorneys at top Boston law firms has stayed generally static — depending on the specialty of the firm — despite

The growth of IP law

One area of law that continues to grow among top firms is intellectual property (IP) law. That's because the business is increasingly driven by unique innovations that require patent protection and other legal attention. IP increasingly is the core asset of emerging companies and requires attorneys with a mix of technical and legal backgrounds. Most of the largest Boston law firms have significant IP practices, and several firms, including Fish & Richardson and Wolf Greenfield, specialize in IP law.

growth in the local economy. The general chill in the legal industry has meant fewer opportunities for young attorneys across the board, making law school a riskier option given the costs involved in obtaining a legal degree.

What lawyers make

Despite the economic pressures on the legal industry, lawyers at the top levels in the industry make big bucks. Top law firm partners bill clients in the range of $800 to $1,000 per hour – and above in some cases. Partners get a share of their firm's profits, which are often $1 million per partner. For example, American Lawyer magazine reported that Ropes & Gray had profits per partner of over $2 million in 2015. The firm is not an outlier: Goodwin Procter had profits per partner of over $1.99 million the same year. Partners often must funnel back some profits into the firm, but those numbers serve as a good proxy for how much attorneys make at the leading firms. Associates (meaning lawyers who are not partners) often start at top Boston law firms at salaries of $140,000, and after five years can be earning, with bonuses, over $250,000 per year.

The legal industry is not defined by only the large firms — midsize and small firms abound, and a quick look at the top 100 law firms in Boston reveals great depth in the legal ecosystem. There are dozens of firms with 20 to 40 attorneys, many specializing in certain practice areas, such as real estate or litigation. Their existence is testament to the great depth of the Boston area economy, for smaller companies shop for legal services that match their budgets — and many good law firms are happy to have clients pay them $300 to $500 per hour.

The large firms distort the reality of lawyer pay. According to the Bureau of Labor Statistics, the average salary for a Boston-area lawyer in 2015 was $164,000. New lawyers, such as those who prosecute criminal cases on behalf of the Commonwealth of Massachusetts as assistant district attorneys, commonly earn under $50,000 per year. Paralegals (there are over 5,000 of them in the Boston area), who help lawyers with research, document preparation, and other matters, make on average $53,500 in 2015, according to federal data.

The Boston area accounting industry

Just as lawyers are essential to business activity, so too are accounting firms. Businesses must turn to accounting firms for a range of services, including taxes, auditing, compliance and business valuation. But unlike the legal industry, accounting is on a tear: The demand for accountants is exceeding the supply, and newly minted accounting graduates generally are finding plenty of opportunities.

The top of the accounting world is defined by the so-called Big Four: PwC, Deloitte, Ernst & Young, and KMPG. All four have offices around the world, and each has a significant presence in Boston. The Big Four in Boston employ over 2,000 certified public accountants, with PwC being the leader with 997. Several other national accounting firms have a presence in Boston, including RSM, Grant Thornton, CBIZ Tofias/Mayer Hoffman McCann, and BDO.

Here are the top 10 accounting firms, in order of Massachusetts CPAs:
(from data in the Boston Business Journal's 2016 top accounting firms list)

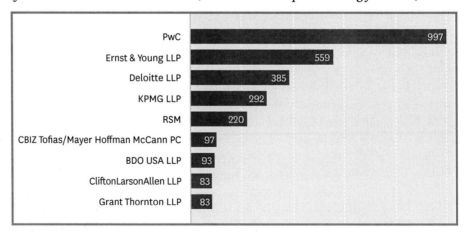

Large publicly held companies usually hire a Big Four firm (or one of the other large national accounting firms, like Grant Thornton and RSM) to do their auditing work. But the Boston area accounting industry, like the legal industry, is very deep, with many regional firms competing for the business of privately held companies of all sizes.

What accountants make

Bureau of Labor Statistics data from 2015 puts the average salary for Massachusetts' 35,000 accountants and auditors at $82,500, although it is fair to say that pay relates to firm size, and managers and more senior people make into the six figures. The demand for accounting talent in Boston puts entry-level salaries at the Big Four above $60,000, according to various sources.

IT consulting

As the technology increasingly pervades business processes, and companies are under pressure to keep up with competitors and also face risks from Internet security, information technology (IT) consultancies have seen strong growth. Large accounting firms have profited from the trend: PwC and Deloitte both have strong IT consulting practices, with over 1,000 IT consultants between them, according to the 2016 Boston Business Journal's list of largest IT consultants. Accenture is the Boston area's largest practice, reporting a total of 1,195 local IT consultants in its Back Bay office. Demand for IT consultants is high, and computer science majors can land starting salaries north of $80,000 per year.

Top IT consultancies also include: Sapient, Eliassen Group, Collaborative Consulting and RSM.

Management consulting

Boston has a wide-ranging group of management consultants, from the classic consulting brands like McKinsey and Co. that offer an array of services to boutique firms that focus strictly on certain disciplines, like talent assessment or employee benefits. Here again firms like PwC and Deloitte, with traditional accounting roots, have a variety of management consulting practices. But it is only natural, given the technological change in business, that business strategy increasingly is integrated with technological strategy. Homegrown consultancies include Charles River Associates, which is publicly traded, Bain and Co., and the Boston Consulting Group. Smaller firms include the Brattle Group, L.E.K. Consulting and the Analysis Group.

Executive recruiting, temp placement

With hiring picking up steam over the past few years, more businesses out-source some recruiting functions to specialty firms, so-called headhunters, to fill top and upper level positions. But given the demand for talent in certain fields, employers are increasingly turning to placement firms for both perma-nent and temporary help. Search firms usually are interested in experienced executives, but with the hot job market, especially for those with tech and finance skills, some placement firms likely would be interested in relatively inexperienced people.

Temporary placement firms are often a good place to test the waters at var-ious companies, and Boston has many temp firms to choose from. Among the largest locally are national firms, including Randstad and Adecco USA. Several temp placement firms focus on IT and engineering placement, including Aerotek in Woburn, Mass.

Some people to know in professional services:

Robert Popeo, the chairman of Mintz Levin, one of the city's top law firms, is considered a valuable adviser on legal and civic matters.

William Bacic, the managing partner for Deloitte in New England, is also active in helping many civic organizations.

Dave MacKeen, CEO of the Eliassen Group, has been driving the tech con-sulting and placement company to fast growth.

George Neble is the Boston office managing partner for Ernst & Young and serves on several boards, including the United Way of Massachusetts Bay.

Amy Pitter, former Commissioner of the state's Department of Revenue, was recently named as the CEO of the Massachusetts Society of Certified Public Accountants.

Bob Boudreau is the CEO of WinterWyman, one of the top executive search and temporary placement firms in the Boston area.

Walter Prince is one of the founders of the law firm Prince Lobel, and the only name partner of a major local law firm who's African American.

Susan Pravda is managing partner of the Boston office of Foley & Lardner and is also managing partner of the firm's venture arm, Foley Ventures LLC.

Susan Murley is co-managing partner of WilmerHale, one of the city's largest law firms.

Advertising, marketing, PR, and media

Few areas of business have gone through as much change in the past 10 years as the marketing and media industries. As communication channels have migrated from newsprint and TV screens to laptops and cell phones, digital marketing and media have steadily eroded the traditional models. New companies have proliferated, and incumbent businesses have adapted or gone away. The prosperity in Greater Boston has been particularly good for advertising and public relations firms, as marketing spending is especially sensitive to the ebbs and flows of the economy. The paradigm shift toward digital platforms is good news for recent grads who live and breathe social media.

Boston has a healthy advertising industry, spawned by the emergence of a handful of successful firms a generation ago, especially Hill Holliday, Arnold Advertising, and MullenLowe. These agencies grew by winning prestigious consumer accounts. For example, Dunkin' Donuts and Bank of America have been with Hill Holliday for many years; JetBlue is a client of MullenLowe's; and Progressive Insurance (featuring the character Flo) commercials are generated by Arnold. But these agencies can only thrive by expanding their repertoire well beyond TV commercials — they all do a significant amount of digital work for their clients.

Boston's largest advertising agency is the Boston office of DigitasLBi, whose name clearly reflects its focus. DigitasLBi is an international firm with roots in Boston. Over 600 of its 6,000 employees work in downtown Boston, and the local office's rapid expansion is a testament to the growth in digital advertising. One of DigitasLBi's top clients is General Motors, a traditional brand that is using new ways (and old) to find customers.

Andrew Graff

"It used to be, there were traditional agencies, there were digital agencies," said Andrew Graff, the CEO of Allen & Gerritsen, a Boston ad agency. "The reality is we're all marketers in the digital world. You have to be versed in all of it."

Top 10 Boston ad agencies ranked by the number of Massachusetts employees:
(as reported by the Boston Business Journal in August 2016)

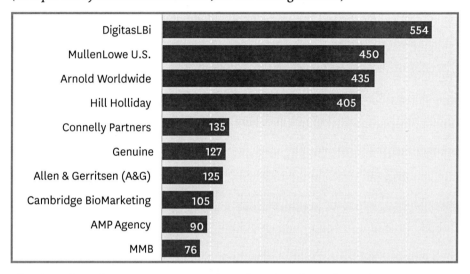

The digital age has meant more technical and analytical people now populate ad agencies, for understanding how to mine new communication platforms and measure the results continue to grow in importance. All the same, Graff said, at his agency, having a sense of adventure and a capacity for risk-taking are important prerequisites.

"We hire on mindset versus skillset, especially when you have a lot of young people. We're not all about creating ads anymore. We can't be," Graff said. "Our business has evolved into the uses of technology for advertising and one-on-one brand experiences. We kind of describe it around here as

uncharted territory is our playground. Advertising has always been like this. You have to do things nobody's done before so you have to be a risk-taker and you have to be comfortable with that. We have a thing around here, we call it 'permission to fail.' Your success is based on putting yourself out there and taking the chance. And if you fail, figure out how to pick up and move on. But success here is not being a holdback or being afraid to put yourself out on a limb."

Public relations

Boston has a healthy public relations industry that is populated mostly with relatively small, independently owned firms of 10 to 50 employees. Some of the largest national firms, such as Weber Shandwick and FleishmanHillard, have significant offices in Boston, but it remains a highly fragmented industry. Like in advertising, the trend in PR is increasingly toward digital services as firms look to deploy the newest platforms to give their clients exposure.

And because of the Boston's region's strong tech and biotech industries, some of the firms have a predominately tech or life sciences client base.

The top 5, in terms of local PR professionals, looks like this:
(from BBJ's Book of Lists)

1. **Weber Shandwick**, a national firm with strong Boston roots.

2. **Racepoint Global**, which was started by Larry Weber after he left Weber Shandwick.

3. **MSL Boston**, a result of the acquisition of Schwartz Communications, a longtime tech PR firm in Waltham.

4. **Cone Communications**, which is made a name for itself in brand communications and cause marketing.

5. **The MullenLowe Group**, primarily an ad agency that also has a significant PR arm.

Boston also has many smaller, successful PR firms, including: Regan Communications Group, Feinstein Kean Healthcare (which focuses on life sciences), two firms, O'Neill and Associates and Rasky Baerlein Strategic Communications, that have a strong public policy focus, and a handful of fast-growing agencies, such as InkHouse.

Public relations success factors

Boston's PR scene is filled with young, ambitious recent college grads, and it takes an assortment of skills to succeed in the industry. Good public relations professionals have to be rabid consumers of news and follow the work of the media relentlessly. They also have to be experts in the art of persuasion, for they must sell their ideas to the media on behalf of their clients. They also have to be comfortable with rejection, as many of their pitches will fall on deaf ears. And of course, more than ever, they have to understand the potential (and peril) of digital media as a communications tool.

Peter Mancusi knows the communications world from many angles. He worked at the Boston Globe for many years, and joined the public relations firm Weber Shandwick in 2002. When asked about what it takes to make it in PR, he had this to say:

Peter Mancusi

"The profile of somebody we look for is obviously somebody who's smart, but creative is a word that comes to mind. Because a lot of the problems and issues that a company has, the solutions to them are not always obvious. And it takes creative people to think about how to better tell somebody's story than they can tell it themselves — and how to navigate issues better than (the clients) could navigate themselves."

"Public relations is not a set of tasks. It's not writing press releases — (although) there is some nuts and bolts work obviously to any sector. People who do best in it are creative people, and we have people now who are video specialists and digital specialists who come up with these amazing ways to promote clients and tell stories in ways the clients could never have dreamed of themselves."

The Boston media scene

Boston's top newspapers and magazines have seen a steady decline in print readers while generally enjoying an increase their digital audiences. Here's the dollars and cents problem for media in the digital revolution: Online ad dollars haven't compensated for the decline of print revenue. While traditional media have adapted to the new era of electronic news, in the past 15 years daily newspapers, including the Boston Globe and Boston Herald, have trimmed down their staffs because of circulation and advertising revenue declines.

That is one reason billionaire John Henry's purchase of the Boston Globe in 2013 was seen as such a positive development for the region's leading daily newspaper. Henry, the principal owner of the Red Sox, has pumped money into new initiatives while trying to fight the tide of declining print circulation and revenue. The longtime competitor of the Globe, the Boston Herald, a splashy tabloid, has survived the digital revolution, albeit with much less newsroom heft than before the Internet took over the news. Pat Purcell, the longtime owner of the Herald, has reduced overhead in other high-cost areas, in particular in printing and distribution, when he worked out a deal with the Globe in 2012 to have the Globe print and deliver his paper.

The Globe's parent company also is the publisher of Boston.com, which is run separately from the Boston Globe (the Globe's website is BostonGlobe.com).

Community newspapers surrounding the city

A large media company, nationwide in scope, owns many Massachusetts daily and weekly newspapers. The parent company is New Media Investment Group, and the largest Massachusetts division is GateHouse Media, publisher of nine daily newspapers and most of the weekly community newspapers in Eastern Massachusetts. New Media also owns several other regional dailies, including the Cape Cod Times and the Worcester Telegram & Gazette. GateHouse is a common first step for recent grads trying to break into journalism.

Other relevant media outlets include BostInno, a digital-only media company that targets a younger demographic with tech and lifestyle news, and the Boston Business Journal, which publishes six daily email editions along with a weekly print edition. If you're looking for day-to-day updates on the local business scene, including news on startups and local growth companies, subscribing to emails from both BostInno and the BBJ makes a lot of sense. The BBJ produces an annual publication, The Book of Lists, a compendium of its weekly research that also serves as a useful tool for learning more about the local economy. It's also an important source of data for this book.

Tech publishing

The Boston area also has some significant tech media companies. One of the largest is International Data Group, a tech research, media and events firm with revenue exceeding $3.8 billion in 2015. IDG publishes titles including CIO, Macworld, Network World and GamePro. International

Data Corporation, or IDC, is an IDG subsidiary that generates market research for the tech industry. Another local tech media company is TechTarget, which operates about 150 websites in various tech niches, including network security and data storage. TechTarget is a public company with revenues of $112 million in 2015.

TV and radio

Boston is ranked as the 7th largest television market in the country, and has a full lineup of local affiliates — stations either owned by or with partnerships with national networks. This link takes you to a full listing of the regional stations, including New Hampshire. stationindex.com/tv/markets/Boston

Boston's public television station, WGBH, is considered one of the most dynamic in the country in part because of its success in creating and distributing original programming. WGBH produces more than two-thirds of the programs the Public Broadcasting Service distributes to its members, including Nova, Frontline, and American Experience. Even though WGBH is a nonprofit, it has positioned itself as a growing enterprise buoyed by syndicating its content.

WGBH also has invested in expanding its local radio news programming, putting it in direct competition with WBUR, one of the region's top radio stations. WBUR not only covers the local market, it also is known nationally for programming it distributes to its sister stations across the country, including On Point, Here & Now, and Only a Game (which is heard on 220 stations). WBZ NewsRadio, found on the AM dial, is a longstanding minute-to-minute news source in Boston.

New England Cable News (NECN) is a locally focused cable news channel that also pays close attention to the regional economy.

Some people to know in advertising, PR and media

Karen Kaplan is the CEO of ad agency Hill Holliday and a leader in civic circles, serving recently as the chairwoman of the Greater Boston Chamber of Commerce.

Micho Spring leads the Boston office of Weber Shandwick and also is the firm's chair of its Global Corporate Practice.

Pam Hamlin is the global president of Arnold Worldwide, the second largest ad agency in Boston.

Beth Monaghan and **Meg O'Leary** are the principals of InkHouse, a fast-growing public relations agency in Waltham, Mass.

Charlie Kravetz is the general manager of WBUR, leading one of the nation's leading public radio stations.

Bill Fine is the president and general manager of WCVB-TV (Channel 5), a perennial ratings leader in the local TV market.

Larry Weber, the founder of Racepoint Global, is considered a thought leader in public relations and is the author of five books on marketing, technology and leadership.

Doug Franklin was named the new CEO of the Boston Globe, effective Jan. 1, 2017. He is the former publisher of the Atlanta Journal-Constitution.

Mike St. Peter is the general manager of New England Cable News, Telemundo and NBC Boston, the new NBC affiliate in the Boston market.

Boston's best-known company brands

Boston has some of the best-known sports franchises in the world, but so too have many of its homegrown brands achieved international renown.

Dunkin' Brands: This ubiquitous coffee shop chain got its start on the South Shore in Quincy in 1948. By 1979, there were 1,000 franchises. Today there are 11,750 stores worldwide — including 3,400 international locations. The company headquarters are in Canton, Mass., and with its Baskin Robbins ice cream franchises, brought in $811 million in revenue in 2015.

New Balance Athletic Shoe goes back to 1906 when it was an arch support company. It's now building a new headquarters in Allston-Brighton, part of a 650,000-square-foot development that includes a new commuter rail station. New Balance brands include PF Flyers, Dunham, and most recently, Rockport. It reported $3.7 billion in sales in 2015.

Reebok is another local global footwear brand with billions in sales. Its headquarters is in Canton, Mass., where approximately 1,000 people work, according to a 2014 Boston magazine story. The brand, acquired by Adidas in 2005, designed the first athletic shoe for women.

Gillette is synonymous with shaving, and the brand, now owned by Procter & Gamble, got its start in Boston in 1901 when King Gillette invented the first safety razor. Gillette was acquired by P&G in 2005 and continues to be a huge moneymaker for its parent company. About 1,300 people work at Gillette's World Shaving Headquarters in South Boston.

Boston Beer and Sam Adams: Boston Beer founder Jim Koch appropriated the name of the famous Revolutionary War-era patriot in creating a brewery powerhouse. When he started the company, Koch walked bar to bar in Boston with a suitcase of his beer; in 2014, the company shipped 4.1 million barrels of product, not all of it beer, as Boston Beer also owns the Twisted Tea and Angry Orchard brands.

Staples: This office supply superstore chain was started in 1986 by Tom Stemberg, who realized the world was lacking a supermarket for office products. The first one opened in Brighton, and now has over 2,000 stores, which are overseen at its Framingham, Mass. headquarters.

Fidelity Investments: Fidelity didn't invent the mutual fund, but it certainly popularized it when personal investing took off in the 1980s. It had $2 trillion in assets under management at the end of 2014, and it aggressively markets its reputation as sensible steward of individuals' assets.

Legal Sea Foods started in Inman Square, Cambridge, by George Berkowitz in 1950 as a fish market. It wasn't until 1968 that the first restaurant was born. As of 2014 there were 34 restaurants as Roger Berkowitz, George's son, has expanded the brand with new concepts.

Bose Corp., the maker of sound systems, was started by Amar Bose, then a professor of electrical engineering at MIT, in 1964. The company, based in Framingham, reported $3.5 billion in revenue in 2015, and employs 3,000 people in Massachusetts.

Ocean Spray is a cooperative of 700 cranberry and other citrus growers that generated $2.2 billion in sales in 2013 from its variety of drinks and fresh and dried fruit. It is based in the heart of Massachusetts' cranberry country, Lakeville-Middleboro, in the southeastern part of the state.

TJ Maxx, **HomeGoods**, and **Marshalls** are among the brands of the TJX Companies, based in Framingham, Mass. TTotal sales topped $30.9 billion in FY 2016 with 3,675 stores and 216,000 employees worldwide.

Wayfair, headquartered in the Back Bay, specializes in home furnishing and décor, and rapidly passed the $2 billion mark in revenue in 2015 and was on track to surpass $3 billion in 2016.

Commercial real estate and the Boston boom

The Boston real estate scene is booming, propelled by strong business growth across many sectors. The skyline of the city is being transformed before our eyes, with several major construction projects in process or about to break ground.

Real estate developers have focused their efforts in several areas of the city: downtown, the area in and near the Financial District; the waterfront area, stretching from the Federal Courthouse to the Marine Industrial Park; the Back Bay, including near Mass. Ave., including a 60-story hotel and residences near the Christian Science Center; and the Fenway area has become a hot spot for new residential and retail buildings.

To get a taste of just how large and potentially lucrative the region's commercial real estate market is, consider the following:

Millennium Tower

- In Boston, city planners have approved a pipeline of development projects valued at more than $4 billion, including everything from new towers to luxury housing to run-of-the-mill expansions and renovations to office, laboratory and industrial properties.

- Five towers are in the process of planning or construction that will exceed 600 feet.

- Approximately 4,000 leases were signed in 2014 that accounted for at least 56 million total square feet.

Boston's building boom is epitomized by one project, Millennium Tower, that has risen in the middle of downtown. It is 625 feet high, contains 1.4 million square feet and has 450 luxury condos. Already a new supermarket, operated by Roche Bros., has opened, marking the ongoing transition of Downtown Crossing into both a residential and business neighborhood.

The Boston real estate ecosystem

Commercial real estate is perhaps the purest form of Darwinism in Greater Boston's economy, and as such there is a pecking order of sorts among the various parties vying for survival. There are the owners — the major employers and institutions that own, occupy and build many of the most significant towers and facilities that dot the local landscape, including Fortune 500 companies. They are deep-pocketed investors. They are universities and hospitals.

As such, owners are at the top of the food chain and offer potentially lucrative rewards to the industry's various players whose jobs involve the planning, construction and leasing of office, research and retail space. Those peripheral parties include:

Landowners with dreams of someday building office parks, apartment complexes and shopping centers.

Management companies who specialize in the maintenance, security and general support of properties housing hundreds if not thousands of workers.

Brokers who stand to earn hefty commissions by filling or finding space on behalf of their clients. And by clients, that means virtually any entity that owns, manages or occupies commercial real estate.

Add in the **architects**, the **construction firms**, the **facilities operators** and **property designers**, and you have an industry that affects tens of thousands of professionals with billions in potential earnings up for grabs.

Among the largest residential projects that have opened or are planned:

- **One Seaport Square,** which is building 832 units just over the Channel in South Boston. Ninety-six of those apartments are slated to be micro-units, less than 450 square feet. It's scheduled to open in 2017.

- **One Congress Residential Tower,** which is part of a bigger development project at Government Center. This tower, which will be 46 stories, will have 475 rental units and is expected to open in 2019.

- **Avalon North Station,** near the TD Boston Garden, will have 503 rental units and be 38 stories tall.

- **AVA Theater District** opened in August, 2015 with 398 rental units. One bedrooms start at $3,074, according to its website (in November, 2015).

- **Pierce Boston** is a 30-story tower in the fast-growing Fenway area. It will have 109 condos and 240 apartments.

The property owners

Ownership of Greater Boston's commercial real estate generally falls into two buckets: Users and investors. Users are the institutions that both own and use the properties they are affiliated with, and they include many of the biggest and most well known companies and nonprofits in the commonwealth. Examples include:

Partners HealthCare, with its world-renowned portfolio of hospitals including Brigham and Women's and Massachusetts General Hospital, is an owner of research and care facilities throughout the state. As of the end of 2014, Partners reported more than $4.7 billion worth of real estate assets on its balance sheet.

State Street Corp., with thousands of portfolio managers, currency and technology analysts and back-office administrators, is an owner of office buildings and data facilities throughout the world. As of 2014, State Street owned more than 1 million square feet of commercial properties, not including another 6.8 million square feet of leased space in major cities in the U.S., Europe, Asia and Latin America.

Harvard University is an owner of student dorms, academic buildings and dining facilities spread throughout its primary 209-acre campus in the heart of the city of Cambridge. As of 2014, Harvard reported more than $465 million in on-campus capital projects and improvements underway, a pipeline of new buildings and renovations that does not include the $5 billion in real estate investments owned by Harvard's $36.4 billion endowment.

In contrast to owner-users, owner-investors are sources of capital — perhaps a sovereign wealth fund, or a real estate investment trust, or a multinational insurance company — that seek to deploy their cash in real estate assets in hopes of generating a robust return. That return can come in one of two forms: a recurring revenue stream in which a property's rental income exceeds its debt service and operating costs; and a cash out, in which a property is sold for more than its acquisition price.

Some firms have made hundreds of millions buying and selling Boston office buildings.

Both operating models present significant upside for savvy investors, many of which dabble in both the recurring revenue and cash-out strategies as market opportunities materialize. That said, it is the cash outs that garner the headlines and solidify the reputations of "legends" within the sector. And for good reason. To wit:

- In 2006, Normandy Real Estate Partners and Five Mile Capital Partners paid approximately $660 million to acquire the John Hancock Tower, Boston's tallest skyscraper, out of a bankruptcy auction. Four years later, it sold the glass tower to Boston Properties for $930 million.

- In 2001, an investment group led by real estate giant Jamestown paid $367 million for the 1.1 million-square-foot, 38-story office tower at One Federal Street in Boston. Five years later, the owners netted a $157 million gain when its sold the very same property to a group affiliated with New York-based Tishman Speyer.

- In 2003, Normandy Partners acquired another Boston tower, 99 Summer St., for around $68 million. After reaping a decade of returns from the well-leased, Class-A tower, Normandy flipped 99 Summer to a subsidiary of Massachusetts Mutual for $110.8 million, or some $42 million more than it originally paid.

So why are owners considered the top of the food chain relative to the various other service providers in commercial real estate? The answer is simple: That's where the money flow begins. The closer and tighter one's ties to a heavy-hitting owner, the better one's prospects are to make a career-long killing in the sector.

The developers

While real estate owners take a more practical, if not scientific, approach to dealing in commercial real estate, developers are the industry's artistic dreamers. In every open field they see office parks. In vacant warehouses, they see condos. Along every major highway and rail line, they see potential for the next live-work-play mega complex.

Developers are to real estate as directors are to Hollywood; they have the vision and the know-how to bring it to life. But that doesn't necessarily mean they have the money to make it happen. Many developers require outside investors as well as partners — perhaps a construction partner, or a land owner — to help get a project off the ground. Still, some have the capital and resources to go it alone. Examples of how these two modes of operation are manifesting in Greater Boston include:

Boston Properties, one of the largest real estate investment trusts in the country, is building a 17-story, 425,000-square-foot office tower in the Back Bay that will ultimately house financial services giant Natixis. With an anchor tenant in hand, and ample cash and access to the public markets, Boston Properties has the resources and expertise to build, lease and manage the 888 Boylston St. property as part of its broader Prudential Center portfolio in the city's Back Bay neighborhood. Boston Properties also has big plans for the North Station/Boston Garden area, a 1.87 million-square-foot development that will include office, retail and approximately 500 residential units.

Developer Joe Fallon has for the better part of the past decade incrementally brought to fruition a $3 billion plan to redevelop a nine-block swath of former industrial and freight parcels in Boston's Seaport District into a state-of-the-art office and residential complex. The series of projects has seen Fallon team with the likes of Vertex Pharmaceuticals, which signed a $1 billion lease to occupy more than 1 million square feet of office and lab space, as well as financiers ranging from the Royal Bank of Scotland to Massachusetts Mutual Insurance Co.

Since acquiring the New England Patriots as well as the real estate connected to its home stadium in Foxborough, Mass., team owner **Robert Kraft** has incrementally expanded its holdings to include a new stadium, an outdoor retail complex as well as medical and hotel facilities. The multi-billion-dollar development was privately funded, although each stage of building has been advanced through a number of savvy agreements with top brands and anchor tenants with the likes of Trader Joe's, CVS Caremark, Bass Pro and Showcase Cinemas.

Alas, all developers need some sort of skin in the game, but it is their dependence on consortiums of investors, service providers and property owners — particularly when it comes to projects of significant scale — that contributes to the complicated and often controversial nature of their efforts. Indeed, while many have successfully threaded the needle to the effect of great financial rewards, many have fallen flat or found themselves mired in years of litigation and great financial losses. Among the more notable difficult projects in recent years:

Westwood Station: A multi-billion-dollar proposal to overhaul empty parcels adjacent to major highways and less than 20 miles from downtown Boston went bust after the 2008 credit crisis. What was once a plan to build out millions of square feet in office, lab, retail and residential spaces quickly fizzled as the economy took a nosedive and financing sources dried up. Owners Cabot, Cabot & Forbes and Connecticut's CommonFund ultimately sold their interests in the site after disagreements that boiled over into the media and courts. Today, the site is slated for a much smaller development under new owners.

Quincy Center: What was billed as the largest urban redevelopment plan in the country quickly fizzled in 2014 when developer StreetWorks conceded that Class A properties wouldn't command Class A rents in the city of Quincy. The proposed $1.6 billion project hinged on buy-in among the state's biggest employers in the life sciences and high technology sectors — something that never came to fruition amid stiff competition from other innovation hubs, namely the red-hot neighborhood of Kendall Square in Cambridge. Despite millions in public infrastructure funding and investment from StreetWorks, the grand plan went belly up in 2014 due to its inability to lure an anchor tenant of any consequence its way.

The high-profile nature of their wins and losses aside, developers are among the most respected players in Greater Boston's real estate scene. They are visionaries. They are opportunistic. And, when successful, they are sources of great wealth for all sorts of service providers who can stay in their good graces.

The commercial brokers

In the battle for dollars in Greater Boston's commercial real estate sector, there is one group of men and women who dominate the front lines above the rest: the brokers.

Far from the local real estate agent with the plastic smile, commercial brokers are part analyst, part salesperson and part hunter. To succeed, they need to anticipate deal-making before it happens and plant many seeds along the way to ensure they are in the right place at the right time when a client is ready to pull the trigger. They are the eyes and ears within the commercial real estate sector, and are paid handsomely for their ability to keep their clients one step ahead of the broader pricing and occupancy trends in the market.

In terms of compensation, brokers eat what they kill.

In terms of compensation, brokers eat what they kill; they only get paid if and when they can sell a building or secure a lease on behalf of a tenant or landlord. Compensation is solely determined by a percentage — often between 5 percent to 10 percent of a deal's value. That said, it is not unusual for a successful broker with a healthy portfolio of clients in any one of Greater Boston's geographic markets to earn upwards of $250,000 to $500,000 per year. But they've got to hustle.

In Massachusetts, brokers generally fall into one of two categories: selling brokers, and leasing brokers. Selling brokers help landlords and investors acquire, sell and in some cases finance commercial properties. Many operate within what are called "institutional sales" teams that have a handful of men and women who specialize in various aspects of a transaction. Some know how to market a property. Others are number crunchers. Still others specialize in pulling together various financing resources to ensure a deal gets done.

Selling brokers often work hand-in-hand — and within the same offices — with leasing brokers, as many of the same clients who buy and sell properties are the same clients who need big tenants to fill vacant spaces in their buildings. Leasing brokers make those deals happen by keeping tabs on the space and major tenants within their respective office or lab markets. Major leases tend to come together years before a big tenant even needs new space, a situation that speaks to the multitude of considerations that a broker must account for when striking a big lease transaction, and they typically last between five and 10 years. As such, leasing brokers typically are paid on a sliding scale — starting at around 7 percent of a lease's annual value and falling to a typical low of 3 percent — over the life of every lease they close.

Top brokerages in Massachusetts, in terms of square feet leased in 2015. All these firms have Boston offices:
(per the Boston Business Journal)

1. **Cushman & Wakefield Inc.** (11.13 million)

2. **CBRE/New England** (11.1 million)

3. **JLL** — (Jones, Lang, LaSalle) (8.42 million)

4. **Transwestern/RBJ** (7.92 million)

5. **Colliers International** (6.2 million)

Top construction companies, followed by the number of Massachusetts employees:
(per the Boston Business Journal's 2016 list of general contractors)

1. **Suffolk Construction** (940 Mass. employees)

2. **Consigli Construction** (600)

3. **Shawmut Design and Construction** (492)

4. **Bond Brothers** (610)

5. **Gilbane Building Co.** (240)

Here are the top architecture firms, in terms of Massachusetts billings:
(per the Boston Business Journal 2016 architectural firm list)

1. **Elkus Manfredi Architects** (320 total staff)

2. **CBT Architects** (225)

3. **Payette** (134)

4. **Stantec** (464)

5. **Gensler** (140)

So how to break in to commercial real estate?

Boston's hotel and restaurant boom

Boston is undergoing a hotel building boom almost as striking as its surge in luxury apartment construction. According to Curbed Boston, a website that tracks real estate news, 4,200 new or renovated rooms are coming online by June, 2017. Among the new hotels are 200 rooms as part of the Four Seasons Hotel and Private Residences at 1 Dalton St., by the Christian Science Center in the Back Bay. That building is slated to be 61 stories and will be among several towers either under construction or planned that will alter the Boston skyline. The new hotels will compete with the likes of Sheraton Boston, the city's largest, with 1,220 rooms; the Boston Marriott Copley Place (1,147 rooms); and the Boston Park Plaza, with 1,054 rooms.

Restaurant jobs are abundant as the Boston area builds on its reputation as a fining dining center. There are 15,000 restaurants in Massachusetts, and only a handful are fully staffed, said Massachusetts Restaurant Association CEO Bob Luz in a recent Boston Business Journal interview. The number of restaurants has grown by 15 percent since 2000. And the number of restaurant jobs was up 20 percent in the same period. In the overall hospital and restaurant sector, the total employment is 298,000 — that's up by 60,000 jobs, or 26 percent.

The real estate industry's tradition of cutthroat competition highlights an emphasis and appreciation for networking skills, information gathering and overall resilience. And at the end of the day, it is the men and women with a nose for value and a knack for arbitrage — the ability to buy low and sell high — who ultimately separate from the pack and attract the kind of capital and resources that continue to dramatically reshape the region's skyline to this day.

The bad news for newcomers to the business is the commercial real estate industry turns on key relationships forged over many years. Market-moving information — everything from major companies seeking more or less space to significant investments in undervalued properties and neighborhoods — is frequently at stake, as are substantial sums of money. The idea that a major client, let alone a developer or brokerage firm, would jeopardize a lucrative deal or key client relationship at the hands of an unproven employee just out of school is a nonstarter.

The good news is there are ample opportunities to break into the business. Virtually all commercial real estate employers have two career tracks that can ultimately lead to a well-compensated, senior position in the industry. The first track is populated by so-called "field personnel." They are the entry-level construction workers at general contracting firms. They are the ambitious "associates" at brokerage firms whose primary tasks upon being hired are largely to spend each day cold-calling, emailing and social-media blitzing as many prospective clients as humanly possible. They are the assistant analysts at development and investment firms who must work long hours visiting properties, crunching numbers and supporting the preparation of research reports concerning the prospects of current and potential projects.

Save for the highly competitive research and analysis positions at investment and development firms, pay for these "field" jobs is generally low — often in the $30,000-to-$40,000 range. That said, the payoff can be fast and substantial for those low-level staffers who can prove themselves as resilient and savvy enough to display a knack to get the job done, particularly when it comes to drumming up new business.

The second track for entry into the commercial real estate business is more in line with large companies in typical office settings. Entry-level accounting positions are numerous, particularly as they apply to businesses that work on a project-to-project basis. Traditional administrative and marketing positions are also key components to many of the largest employers in commercial real estate, although their availability is closely tied to the health of what is one of the most reliably cyclical industries. Those jobs are the last to be added when times are good, and the first to disappear when the economy stalls.

Compensation for these "office" tracks is on par with those in competing sectors of the economy.

As to what commercial real estate firms are looking for when it comes to hiring men and women out of college, the answer among most firms is often the same: They want people from recognizable schools who display the right mix of personality, professionalism and competitive fire. In short, they want people who can someday grow and assume senior leadership positions to run their business.

Some people to know in Boston real estate:

Stephen Karp, one of the pivotal developers on in the region, runs New England Development, which has specialized in shopping centers but has expanded into hotel ownership and residential development, including Pinehills, south of Boston, and more recently, Pier 4 on the Boston waterfront.

Joe Fallon is responsible for developing an assortment of office and residential properties on the Boston waterfront near the Federal Courthouse.

John Fish is one of Boston's most famous businessmen, a leader in philanthropic circles and the catalyst for Boston's failed bid for the Olympics. He is the CEO of Suffolk Construction, the most successful construction firm in Boston.

Steve Samuels is the founder of Samuels & Associates and is one of the forces transforming the Fenway neighborhood with new residential and retail projects. One of his projects, Van Ness, will be a 172-unit building.

Andy Hoar, co-managing partner at brokerage firm CBRE/New England with Kevin Doyle, leads the largest brokerage firm in the region.

David Begelfer is the CEO of Boston's leading real estate trade group, NAIOP Massachusetts, and one of the area's most knowledgeable experts on commercial real estate trends.

John Drew of the Drew Company was an early leader in developing the South Boston waterfront area, and his most recent project, a 236-unit luxury building called Waterside Place, recently opened.

Rob Griffin recently left the capital markets group at Cushman & Wakefield for Newmark Grubb Knight Frank, a competing real estate brokerage firm. He's considered one of the top brokers in selling premium commercial properties in Boston.

Tom O'Brien, founding partner and managing director of HYM Investment Group and former head of the Boston Redevelopment Authority, is the force behind one of the biggest projects in Boston, the creation of a six-building, 2.3-million-square-foot project at the site of the Government Center Garage near Faneuil Hall.

Bill Cummings is one of the Boston area's legendary developers and property managers, having built or redeveloped 10 million square feet in suburban Boston at his namesake firm. He and his wife Joyce decided to give away their wealth through the creation of a $1 billion foundation.

Douglas Linde is the president of Boston Properties, a Boston-based real estate investment trust with holdings in Boston and three other cities: New York, Washington D.C. and San Francisco. Boston Properties has been aggressive as an owner and developer in Boston, and is planning a large project in the North Station area.

Brian Golden is the director of the Boston Planning and Development Agency (formerly called the Boston Redevelopment Authority), the city agency that regulates development. Part of his responsibility is helping facilitate the creation of Mayor Marty Walsh's goal of building more middle-income and affordable housing for Boston residents.

PART THREE

Boston's economic challenges and opportunities

The ultimate economic advantage: Greater Boston's university system

Boston's decades-long renaissance has been the envy of virtually every city in the United States, with its frothy job market and rapid wealth creation rooted in an innovative, research-driven economy. Yet those fruits stem from one of the region's oldest and, increasingly, one of its more vulnerable assets: a world-renowned cluster of colleges and universities.

The roots of the Greater Boston economy are largely defined by the dozens of academic institutions that dot its urban neighborhoods and encompass swaths of acreage in its bucolic suburbs. In some respects the region can be viewed simply as a collection of college towns that throw off billions in economic activity, spawn cutting-edge startups and annually draw hundreds-of-thousands of students, including a fast-expanding number from abroad, each year. The Massachusetts tally of higher ed students is 594,000 (as of 2013), with the bulk of those in Boston and environs.

As employers, local schools boast many of the largest payrolls in the state, with Harvard University alone supporting a workforce of some 16,000 people. Jobs in academia can run from the obvious (faculty and administration) to the cutting edge (medical research and robotics), from the mundane (maintenance and food services) to the lucrative (asset management and real estate development). It is a sector that is every bit a microcosm of the region's innovation economy.

And yet higher ed, for all of its tradition and centuries of positive influence on the region, is hurting. Demographic trends are not in its favor, both in terms of population growth in the Northeast and the pipeline of college-age students expected to descend on its campuses over the next decade. Easy access to capital prior to the 2008 credit crash prompted many institutions to borrow heavily in support of new classroom facilities and student dorms — only to burden those very same colleges and universities with debt loads that, given enrollment trends, that will be challenging to sustain for the long term. Layoffs and job losses through attrition have become the norm at even the most prestigious schools in the land — Harvard and Wellesley College, to name two — let alone the dozens of pricey, lower-tier private colleges that have increasingly struggled to provide a value proposition to prospective students.

Alas, most institutions are taking a proactive approach. Some schools are adapting through technology, particularly online learning, while others are doubling down on core strengths. Still others are seeking new revenue opportunities through partnerships, expanded academic offerings and flexible degree tracks to remain relevant and head off the doomsday scenarios that have already claimed some of their industry peers.

How the industry will respond to its challenges is still a work in progress. But, no surprise, change is coming.

Positive returns: The economic payoff of research and on-campus innovation

Higher ed's economic impact in Massachusetts is difficult to quantify, partly because the area's collection of private schools largely operate as nonprofits with limited reporting requirements. At the same time, the commonwealth's system of public universities and colleges operate as an extension of the state, with some of its spending and revenue dictated by the legislative budget process. In short, the vast majority of these institutions, unlike for-profit companies, are slow to report their most vital statistics, and they generate little-to-no tax revenue for their local communities, let alone the commonwealth.

Higher ed's payoff to Boston almost defies measurement, although MIT has put numbers to its own impact.

Nonetheless, higher ed's payoffs to the state is significant. A recent study by the Massachusetts Institute of Technology makes the case that while many colleges and universities provide little tax benefit to the state, their emphasis on research and innovation have proven a boon when it comes to job creation. At MIT alone, where more than half of its $3.18 billion in 2014 revenue was derived from research and development, alumni as of 2009 were credited with running an estimated 6,900 Massachusetts companies with worldwide sales of roughly $164 billion. That was around 26 percent of all sales recorded by Bay State businesses that year.

All told, Massachusetts companies run by MIT grads employed around 1 million as of the survey year, a number that no doubt has grown amid a local explosion in new technology and life sciences jobs since the study's publication.

MIT is not alone in spawning successful businesses and the leaders who run them. Indeed, many have followed its path by launching programs in entrepreneurship as well as hosting incubator space to house and support potentially lucrative research efforts that take root on campus. Count lesser-known schools such as Worcester Polytechnic Institute, Merrimack College, Western New England College and Bentley University among the growing list of institutions to have carved out startup space and related resources for students and faculty alike.

But different schools have different objectives when it comes to influencing and even reshaping the U.S. economy. The Fortune 500 is littered with CEOs who graduated from Harvard Business School, long respected as a catalyst for new and more effective management concepts, while schools such as Babson College in Wellesley and Northeastern University in Boston have fostered global brands by making entrepreneurship a key ingredient in their curriculum. The payoff has been a slew of major Massachusetts employers with Babson and Northeastern roots, companies ranging from data-storage giant EMC Corp. in Hopkinton to consulting powerhouse Accenture.

Universities as wealth managers and property developers

While most colleges and universities operate as nonprofits, their collective wealth is a key driver of economic activity throughout the state. Start with endowments, the pools of assets that schools compile from outside donors, wealthy alumni and gains from investments. These funds total in the tens-of-billions in Massachusetts alone and, if large enough, can supplement a school's operations far and above what can be afforded from traditional tuition payments by students.

Most of the top-performing schools in Massachusetts also are its wealthiest, from an endowment standpoint. The reason for this is simple: it is generally the best schools that can recruit the strongest students with the highest likelihood of attaining career success … which they can then redirect back to their alma mater in the form of philanthropic giving. It is an approach that has snowballed for the likes of Harvard, MIT, Boston College and others that have managed to harness the wealth creation of their alumni, which in turn has helped them become even more selective in whom they invite to populate their campuses.

The largest endowments among colleges and universities in Massachusetts*

	SCHOOL	ENDOWMENT
1	Harvard University	$36.4 billion
2	MIT	$12.4 billion
3	Boston College	$2.2 billion
4	Amherst College	$2.15 billion
5	Williams College	$2.15 billion
6	Smith College	$1.76 billion
7	Tufts University	$1.63 billion
8	Boston University	$1.55 billion
9	Wellesley College	$1.18 billion
10	Northeastern University	$779 million
11	Brandeis University	$766 million
12	Holy Cross	$726 million
13	Mount Holyoke	$713 million
14	Worcester Polytechnic Institute	$416 million
15	Clark University	$392 million
16	Olin College of Engineering	$380 million
17	Babson College	$332 million
18	Berklee College of Music	$321 million
19	Bentley University	$258 million
20	Wheaton College	$193 million

As of 2014 fiscal year-end

Such large pools of wealth require entire teams to manage them, and as such universities tend to be among the most innovative when it comes to hiring people who specialize in allocating capital to a wide range of diverse investment options. For example, Harvard Management, the endowment arm for Harvard University, has long been considered a pioneer when it comes to diversifying its holdings, and is frequently ahead of the curve when it comes to testing new investment strategies, whether they be hedge funds or real estate plays or private equity deals in developing countries.

In recent decades, many schools have sought to build upon their real estate wealth through aggressive land acquisition and development, albeit with mixed results.

But higher ed's wealth spreads far beyond the ledgers of its endowment portfolios, as many schools were founded with gifts that still account for the greatest portion of their net worth today: their campuses. Scan the balance sheet of virtually every school in the commonwealth, and you are likely to find an estimated value for land and property that far outweighs other assets on its books. At Boston University, the value of land and property owned was around $2.1 billion as of mid-2014. At Williams College it was more than $442 million as of last year, while at Tufts University it was $833 million.

At the Franklin Olin College of Engineering in Needham, where the school now operates on 70 acres of land donated by its founders, real estate accounts for about a quarter of its balance sheet.

In recent decades, many schools have sought to build upon their real estate wealth through aggressive land acquisition and development, albeit with mixed results. For example, Boston College, which has long struggled to grow within the confines of its primary campus footprint, has in recent years agreed to pay roughly $200 million to acquire nearly 100 acres near or adjacent to its campus. Plans for at least $400 million in new dorms, academic facilities and related projects are slated for the years ahead.

At Boston University and Northeastern University, decades of land accumulation along some of the city's busiest corridors have been parlayed into development projects aimed to house more students and programs in state-of-the-art facilities. The aim of those ongoing efforts, which were valued last year at more than $288 million at BU and $177 million at NU, has been to boost the institutions' academic standing and recruiting clout.

The development bug also has spread to smaller schools such as the Berklee College of Music, which recently completed a new $100 million dorm and academic project, to public institutions including the University of Massachusetts, where capital projects are scheduled to total in the billions over the next 10 years.

Higher education pays ... for some

Top decision makers — i.e. CEOs — at America's largest public companies have been pilloried in recent years for compensation that critics say is misaligned with values and ethics of good citizenship, let alone the average paycheck of a typical employee. But little is said about the hefty paydays collected by the men and women whose offices populate the ivory towers of academia, an industry that has its fair share of compensation challenges to grapple with.

While million-dollar compensation packages are common for leaders running some of the largest and most prestigious schools in Massachusetts, meager pay scales for the growing legions of higher ed's corps of part-time faculty — so-called adjuncts — has caught the eye of organized labor.

The reasons for using adjuncts can vary. For example, it can be a relatively risk-free way for an institution to try out a new course, or to see if a given adjunct has the chops to teach at the college level. But for many schools, a heavy reliance on adjuncts usually boils down to a simple equation: such positions are a low-cost option at a time of increased financial pressure for many colleges and universities.

The nation's labor unions have taken note. Since 2014, several schools have seen their part-time teachers, many of whom earn less than $5,000 per semester to teach a course, vote in favor of unionization to improve their negotiating leverage with school administrators. Among the schools to see adjuncts unionize in recent months are Northeastern, Tufts University, Boston University and Lesley University.

The largest employers among colleges and universities in Massachusetts

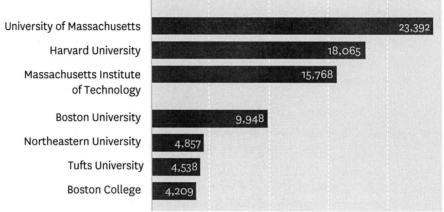

University of Massachusetts	23,392
Harvard University	18,065
Massachusetts Institute of Technology	15,768
Boston University	9,948
Northeastern University	4,857
Tufts University	4,538
Boston College	4,209

Source: Boston Business Journal

Higher ed's pressure points: Enrollment and the price of admission

Ask local college presidents about what keeps them up at night, and their answers are likely to be near identical: negative enrollment trends.

A combination of low birth rates and a demographic shift in favor of the nation's cheaper, warmer states has proven a devastating one-two punch for the pricey private colleges that populate Massachusetts. Many have experienced consecutive years of enrollment declines that show little sign of letting up in the decade ahead, which means many have taken direct hits to their biggest source of revenue: tuition.

At Simmons College in Boston, enrollment tumbled 12 percent between 2009 and 2013. Suffolk University in Boston reported an 8 percent campus-wide decline in 2014, while a slew of others including Boston Architectural College in Boston, Lesley University in Cambridge and Assumption College in Worcester also reported declines in recent years.

Some schools, including Stonehill College in Easton, have even intentionally lowered enrollment rates to better prepare for the steady population declines predicted in the near term. The goal, they say, is to keep costs and resources aligned with the reality that, with enrollment flat or falling, revenue growth will remain a challenge for the foreseeable future.

The largest colleges and universities in Massachusetts, by enrollment

(Full-time equivalent enrollment as reported in fiscal 2014 annual reports)

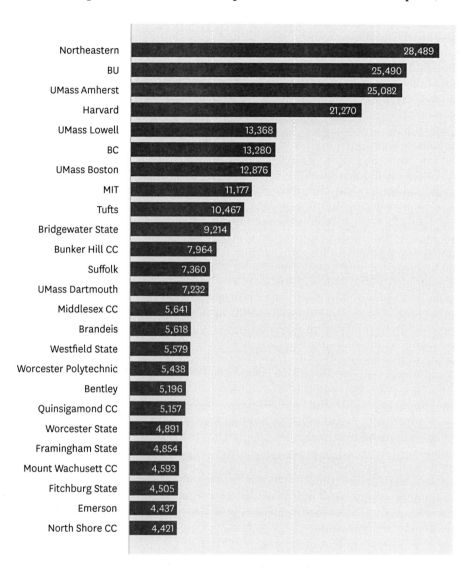

Northeastern	28,489
BU	25,490
UMass Amherst	25,082
Harvard	21,270
UMass Lowell	13,368
BC	13,280
UMass Boston	12,876
MIT	11,177
Tufts	10,467
Bridgewater State	9,214
Bunker Hill CC	7,964
Suffolk	7,360
UMass Dartmouth	7,232
Middlesex CC	5,641
Brandeis	5,618
Westfield State	5,579
Worcester Polytechnic	5,438
Bentley	5,196
Quinsigamond CC	5,157
Worcester State	4,891
Framingham State	4,854
Mount Wachusett CC	4,593
Fitchburg State	4,505
Emerson	4,437
North Shore CC	4,421

Net tuition revenue at many institutions has followed enrollment trends, falling year-over-year in fiscal 2014 at schools including Suffolk, Lesley and Simmons. Even schools that have not experienced enrollment declines, including some of the state's most competitive schools, have struggled to balance their books as they increasingly deploy financial aid as a recruiting tool to draw and retain students on campus. Examples include schools such as such as Wellesley College (51 percent of total tuition and fee revenue) and Wheaton College (46 percent), both of which have been confronted with difficult financial choices in recent years despite steady enrollment trends.

As to why these challenges have been particularly acute among schools in Massachusetts, the reasons are varied. For one, many borrowed heavily to keep pace with an industry-wide investment in state-of-the-art academic facilities and student resources — everything from dorms to dining halls — intended to boost national rankings and recruiting prowess among prospective students. Others saw opportunity in loading up on programs and bloated curricula that better enabled them to be all things to all students — again, with the goal of boosting enrollment on campus. Both factors contributed to a steady rise in the price of admission.

With its world-renowned brand in education, Massachusetts has proven an easy sell to foreign students hoping to study in the United States.

At a time when many families are struggling to rationalize the cost of college, the high-priced lower-tier schools of the Northeast have found themselves in financial straights as more and more students gravitate to lower cost options out of state and within the commonwealth's network of public college and university systems.

Those factors have pushed many schools to look outside of Massachusetts and, increasingly, outside of the United States for students to populate their campuses. Targeted populations have tended to be students from wealthy families in South America and Asia, particularly China.

And with its world-renowned brand in education, Massachusetts has proven an easy sell to foreign students hoping to study in the United States. In each of the five years leading up to 2014, Massachusetts colleges and universities reported a 47 percent increase in the number of foreign-born students on their campuses. That rate of growth was roughly 50 percent greater than the 31 percent expansion in foreign enrollment reported nationally over the same span, according to the Institute of International Education.

Some schools have benefited more than others. For example, Northeastern said foreign enrollment more than tripled between 2009 and 2014 to roughly 2,500 students. At Suffolk, it more than doubled over that same span to around 1,100 students. At Boston College, enrollment among students from

China alone grew to 140 in 2014, up from only three a decade earlier.

Even at the University of Massachusetts system, enrollment among students from China increased nearly 70 percent to over 600 students in the five-year span leading into the 2014 academic year.

The next-generation of Mass. manufacturing: Challenges in a still strong sector

For many, the manufacturing industry conjures up images of dirty, monotonous and sometimes thankless blue-collar jobs, a sector in steep and perpetual decline. In America, it's considered by some as a dead-end career move for young workers, as companies "off-shore" their manufacturing operations to other lower-cost, developing countries.

That's the image of manufacturing. But it's not the reality in Massachusetts and other parts of the country.

Many manufacturing jobs increasingly require bachelor's degrees in fields like engineering, computer design and software writing.

Increasingly, many American corporations are "re-shoring" manufacturing jobs back to the U.S., as new technologies usher in an age of so-called "advanced manufacturing" that relies more heavily on computer-assisted machinery, laser-guided equipment, robotics, 3-D printing, biological-manufacturing and other innovations that require highly skilled workers, researchers and managers.

Many of those jobs increasingly require bachelor's degrees in engineering, computer design, software writing, chemistry, biology and other "STEM" (Science, Technology, Engineering, and Mathematics) fields. To oversee manufacturing operations, companies also need non-STEM college graduates to fill other critical white-collar positions, ranging from financial analysts to human resources personnel to accountants.

In Massachusetts, experts say the state is in particularly good shape to take advantage of this manufacturing trend, due to the its large number of higher-education institutions and a well-educated and trained workforce.

"I'm very optimistic about the future of manufacturing in Massachusetts," says Barry Bluestone, an economist and director of Northeastern University's Dukakis Center for Urban and Regional Policy. Bluestone and his Northeastern colleagues have now conducted two major studies about the future of manufacturing in Massachusetts, both of which point to an encouraging future for the broadly defined sector, which can range from companies making firearms (such as Springfield's Smith & Wesson Corp.) to firms producing sophisticated biopharmaceutical products (such as Cambridge's Genzyme Corp.).

Indeed, Bluestone estimates that 100,000 manufacturing jobs will likely open up in Massachusetts over the next 10 years, as Baby Boomers start to retire in droves. As a result, there's a distinct possibility of a major manufacturing labor shortage in coming years, he warns.

An equally surprising finding by Bluestone: About two-thirds of soon-to-be available jobs will be non-production positions that often require college degrees and up. The front-line production jobs will still continue to require workers with high school or associate's degrees, but the manufacturing sector is also in desperate need of all sorts of workers with more advanced degrees, Bluestone emphasized.

To be sure, the overall Massachusetts manufacturing sector may likely contract in coming years, in terms of total jobs, as it has in recent decades. But the availability of actual jobs should increase due to the expected large number of upcoming retirements, Bluestone said.

Job demand intensifying

The state's manufacturing sector once stood at a peak of about 650,000 workers in the 1960s, but has fallen to about 250,000 today, similar to trends across the rest of the nation. Still, the total manufacturing workforce has largely stabilized over the past few years, thanks largely to the positive "re-shoring" and advanced manufacturing trends, Bluestone said.

Some Massachusetts firms are already feeling the labor-shortage pinch due to retiring employees.

"We have more work than we can currently handle," said Michael Tamasi, chief executive officer at Avon-based AccuRounds Inc., which makes high-end mechanical components for a wide variety of industries. Ten years ago,

AccuRounds employed only 40 people in Massachusetts, but it has grown to about 75 employees in recent years, thanks mainly to advanced manufacturing trends in Massachusetts.

But AccuRounds can't expand much more without additional skilled employees, Tamasi said. "As the sophistication of the industry continues to advance, so does the need for all types of workers, including college-degree employees."

An example of the broad spectrum of jobs available in manufacturing can be found at Milford-based Waters Corp., the publicly traded developer and manufacturer of science technologies for laboratories. Recently, its website was advertising job openings for a synthesis production operator in Taunton, a financial analyst in Milford, a senior applications support scientist in Beverly, and a senior mechanical engineer in Milford.

In particular, the state's highly respected life-science sector has been a big driver of the manufacturing renaissance in Massachusetts.

The largest manufacturer in Massachusetts today, according to state figures, is Lake Region Medical, a Wilmington maker of sophisticated equipment and components for the medical-device sector. Not all of Lake Region's 5,000 jobs in Massachusetts are in front-line production, but the company, which was acquired by Greatbatch in 2015, has a huge number of manufacturing-related engineers and scientists working on all sorts of products in the Bay State.

In general, most life-science companies have their manufacturing operations in Eastern Massachusetts, such as Lake Region and Genzyme Corp.'s manufacturing facility in Framingham. They want to keep such facilities close to their R&D operations and major universities, such as MIT, Harvard, Tufts, Boston University and others.

But as lab and manufacturing spaces in Eastern Massachusetts fill up, companies are increasingly looking further west to base their operations, officials say. In recent years, Bristol-Myers Squibb has spent $750 million on a new bulk-manufacturing plant in Devens, employing nearly 600 people at the former U.S. military base in central Massachusetts.

Recently, General Electric Healthcare set up major operations in Marlborough, near Interstate 495, where it plans to make bioreactors and fermenters for the life-sciences sector.

Now even available lab and sophisticated manufacturing spaces in central Massachusetts are starting to dry up, due to the burgeoning demand for industrial space along Interstate 495, according to Bryan Blake, president of Calare Properties, a commercial real estate firm specializing in buying and managing industrial properties.

"Many of the large manufacturing facilities ... are like big laboratories. They're very clean and sophisticated."

— Peter Abair

"The demand for lab, R&D and manufacturing space has gone way up," Blake said. "It's all driven by the higher skills set of the state's workforce."

Also within the life sciences sector, a particularly strong area has been "biologic manufacturing," or the creation of cells for actual drug products and R&D. A number of biologic facilities are now strewn throughout eastern and central Massachusetts.

In Worcester, the publicly traded AbbVie Inc. has a large biologics and contract-manufacturing operation in the city, which is also home to the respected and growing University of Massachusetts Medical School and UMass Medical Center.

Peter Abair, executive director of MassBioEd, a nonprofit foundation dedicated to developing a talented biotechnology workforce in the state, said all signs point to a further expansion of bio-manufacturing in Massachusetts.

"The technology is changing all the time and companies need skilled workers," said Abair, whose foundation is affiliated with the Massachusetts Biotechnology Council. "Many of the large manufacturing facilities we're talking about are like big laboratories. They're very clean and sophisticated."

Peter Russo, a program manager at Massachusetts Manufacturing Extension Partnership (MEP), said yet another promising area for manufacturing in the state is the clean energy sector. In recent years, Russo has helped young people start new cleantech companies out of Somerville's Greentown Labs, which touts itself as an incubator for "hardware startups."

Russo, who used to own a products development company in Massachusetts, said young people at Greentown Labs are working on everything from propane-gas tank sensors to landfill methane monitors. He's said there's almost a yearning among many young people to make actual tangible products in non-office settings — with many of those young holding college degrees and up. They most definitely don't want to be paper shufflers.

"Manufacturing is changing so fast," said Russo, who has also taught at Babson College. "It's changing who's making products and who they're making it for."

Massachusetts also remains home to many traditional manufacturing firms and operations, from General Electric's hundreds of workers at its jet-engine plant in Lynn to New Balance Athletic Shoe Inc.'s 500 workers at manufacturing facilities in Lawrence and Brighton.

Other manufacturers headquartered in Massachusetts, even though they don't always have a manufacturing presence in the state, include Gillette Co., Bose Corp., Reebok International, Converse, Polar Beverages, and papermaker Crane & Co.

Brian Gilmore, executive vice president of external affairs at Associated Industries of Massachusetts, said all manufacturers face challenges in Massachusetts, including the high cost of living here, especially the region's sky-high prices for electricity.

But he said manufacturers remain here for the same reason that other firms do: For the stream of talented workers coming out of the area's highly regarded high schools, colleges and universities.

"There are plenty of jobs for both high school and college grads," Gilmore said. "The perception of manufacturing is slowly changing. It's getting a much, much better buzz these days."

Made in Massachusetts

A sampling of products that are manufactured in the state

Crane & Co. — The currency paper for the U.S. Treasury is made in Dalton, Mass.

New Balance — Athletic shoes made in Boston and Lawrence.

Gillette Co. — Razors, razor blades are made in South Boston.

Smith & Wesson — Firearms, from pistols to rifles, are made in Springfield, Mass.

Boston Beer Company — Maker of Samuel Adams craft beers has a small brewery in Jamaica Plain.

Joseph Abboud Manufacturing Corp. — makes men's clothing in New Bedford, Mass.

Randolph Engineering — makes eyewear in Randolph, Mass.

Raytheon Co. — Defense contractor and maker of everything from radar equipment to the MIM-104 Patriot anti-missile system, has a manufacturing facility in Tewksbury, Mass.

Durkee-Mower Inc. — Maker of Marshmallow Fluff, the gooey marshmallow crème product, is located in Lynn, Mass.

Genzyme — This biotech, now a division of Sanofi, makes several drugs at its Allston facility.

The New England Confectionery Co., or NECCO, makes the famous Necco Wafers, as well as Sweetheart Conversation Hearts, in Revere, Mass.

Minorities in Boston business:
Leaders and resources

Despite the gains Boston has made over the past few decades as a more diverse, welcoming and international city, there aren't many prominent minority leaders in the upper echelons of the largest corporations. There is, however, more minority power at the top in various nonprofit sectors, especially education. While many local companies engage in significant diversity initiatives, progress in having the white-collar workforce reflect the general population has been slow. Human resources executives say recruiting executives of color from outside the state traditionally has been a challenge. One reason: A generation ago, the city made national headlines during a period when, to achieve school integration goals, students were bussed out of their home districts. It caused an uproar, and images of schoolchildren in buses that were being pelted by rocks from angry mobs became ingrained on the national consciousness. That was in the mid-1970s, and although much has changed in Boston, the city still suffers from the perception that it's not welcoming to minorities.

The executive suites of the region's largest companies are occupied predominately by white males. It's no different in the legal industry. The national association of law placement figures put the percentage of minority law partners in Boston (3.8 percent) at about half the national average. The percentage of black law partners is under 1 percent. It's fair to say that minorities are vastly unrepresented in tech. Where there is relatively strong representation is higher ed. Three local colleges (Emerson, Wheelock, and Cambridge College) are led by African Americans. MIT is led by a native of Venezuela.

Boston has several organizations devoted to executives of color, and none is more prominent than The Partnership, a nonprofit that does training and consulting to further diversity goals. The Partnership is a place for local executives (and entry-level workers) of color to connect and develop leadership and other professional skills. It is led by Carol Fulp, a longtime executive at John Hancock, who said in a 2013 Boston Globe interview that The Partnership helps minority execs navigate complex organizations. "What's most interesting is to see the commonality of interest and the commonality of challenges across ethnic backgrounds. Frequently these are high-potential individuals who are doing well in their organization, but they may be lonely so The Partnership provides a community for them," she said.

ALPFA's mission is "empower and develop Latino men and women as leaders of character for the nation."

Another prominent group for minority business professionals is the local chapter of ALPFA, the Association of Latino Professionals in Finance and Accounting. ALPFA's mission is "empower and develop Latino men and women as leaders of character for the nation, in every sector of the global economy." The local chapter is strong and active, holding many networking events over the course of the year.

There's also a program for Hispanic professionals called Conexion. The program is a 10-month-long experience in which Conexion pairs mid-career Hispanic professionals with experts in diverse fields who serve as executive mentors. Over the last 10 years, Conexion has shaped many Latino leaders in the area. The group's founder and executive director, Phyllis Barajas, is a Latina pioneer herself. She was as the first Latina assistant dean for human resources at the Harvard Kennedy School of Government and served as deputy assistant secretary in the U.S. Department of Education's offices of elementary, secondary, and bilingual education in the Clinton administration.

One local organization is not only working to advance the goals of diversity, it also is attempting to measure the number of minorities in the local workplace. The Commonwealth Compact, which operates out of UMass Boston, has issued reports on diversity numbers from business participants in its surveys. And while the numbers are not scientific, in part because of the self-selection of the institutions providing the data, they reveal there's a much larger percentage of minority hiring in the nonprofit sectors, like government and health care, than in for-profit industries. The latest report, issued in 2013 states: "Blacks were 11 percent of the total sample of workers, but had a much higher presence in the not-for-profit sector, at 16 percent. They were also overrepresented in the government (14 percent) and health care (12 percent) sectors. They were underrepresented in the education sector, 6 percent, and made up only 4 percent in the for-profit sector."

Some minority leaders in the Boston business and civic scene:

Former Gov. Deval Patrick, who left office in early 2015 after eight years as governor, is the best-known African American political figure in Massachusetts. Since leaving office, he has joined Bain Capital as a partner, where he plans to focus on social impact investing.

Diane Patrick, the wife of Deval Patrick, has had a successful career in labor and employment law as a co-managing partner at one of Boston's most prominent law firms, Ropes & Gray.

Bennie Wiley, former CEO of The Partnership, runs her own consulting company, the Wiley Group and serves on many local boards, including Blue Cross Blue Shield of Massachusetts and Boston College.

Flash Wiley, husband of Bennie Wiley, is of counsel at Morgan, Lewis & Bockius. Wiley is a benefactor at Crispus Attucks Children's Center, a founding member of the Harvard Law School and the Harvard Kennedy School Black Alumni organizations.

Carol Fulp is the CEO of The Partnership and previously was the Senior Vice President of Corporate Responsibility and Brand Initiatives at John Hancock Financial, where she oversaw a $12 million philanthropic giving program.

Lee Pelton has been president of Emerson College since 2011, and his local civic involvement includes the Museum of African American History, the Association of Independent Colleges and Universities in Massachusetts, the Boston Municipal Research Bureau, and the Boston Arts Academy.

Keith Motley is the chancellor at UMass Boston and a founder of the Roxbury Preparatory Charter School and chair emeritus of the school's Board of Trustees. He is also the founder and education chair of Concerned Black Men of Massachusetts, Inc., and the Paul Robeson Institute for Positive Self-Development.

Corey Thomas is the president and CEO of Rapid7, a cybersecurity software firm based in downtown Boston that went public in July 2015. The company employs about 600 people.

Ralph Martin is senior vice president and general counsel of Northeastern University, former managing partner of the Boston office of Bingham McCutchen, and was Suffolk County District Attorney from 1992-2002. He also is chairman of the board of The Partnership.

Darnell Williams is the president and CEO of the Urban League of Eastern Massachusetts, a civil rights organization that helps provide education and job training.

Michael Curry is the president of the Boston branch of the National Association for the Advancement of Colored People (NAACP), which has about 1,000 local members.

Robert Lewis Jr. is the executive director of The Base, a nonprofit in Boston that combines sports and academics to help transform the lives of black and Latino boys.

Tito Jackson is the District 7 councilor of Boston, representing Roxbury and parts of Dorchester, the South End, and Fenway.

Ayanna Pressley is the first woman of color ever elected to the Boston City Council. As an at-large councilor, she serves all of Boston.

Steven Wright is the executive partner overseeing the law firm Holland & Knight's Boston office.

Colette Phillips founded and runs her own public relations firm, Colette Phillips Communications, and organizes "Get Konnected," an event series to bring together professionals from diverse backgrounds.

Clayton Turnbull is president of the Waldwin Group and owner of 17 Dunkin' Donuts franchises in Boston.

Ralph de la Torre is the president and CEO of Steward Health Care Systems, Massachusetts' second largest group of hospitals, employing 17,000.

Georgianna Melendez is the executive director of the Commonwealth Compact, an organization that promotes diversity in Boston.

L. Rafael Reif is the president of the Massachusetts Institute of Technology. A native of Venezuela, Reif joined the MIT faculty in 1980 and became president in 2012.

Walter Prince, a native of Boston, is an attorney who founded the law firm Prince Lobel. The firm participates in a number of diversity and workforce initiatives.

Wayne Budd, former U.S. Attorney for the Boston district and general counsel for John Hancock Insurance, now is senior counsel at the law firm Goodwin Procter.

Melvin Miller founded the Bay State Banner in 1965 — and recently celebrated 50 years in business.

Ronald Walker is the secretary of Labor and Workforce Development for the Commonwealth of Massachusetts.

Deborah Jackson is the president of Cambridge College.

Felix Arroyo, a former Boston city councilor, is the head of Health and Human Services for the city of Boston.

Phyllis Barajas is the founder and executive director of Conexión, a decade-old leadership and mentoring program for mid-career Latino professionals in Boston.

Enrique Caballero is the executive director of the Joslin Latino Diabetes Initiative.

Vanessa Calderón-Rosado is the CEO of Inquilinos Boricuas en Acción — IBA — one of the most, if not the most, prolific Latino nonprofits in Boston. The organization was born in the late 60s out of anti-gentrification efforts in the South End. IBA then developed Villa Victoria, an affordable housing complex.

Alberto Calvo is the president of Compare Supermarkets, a Latino family owned chain of neighborhood grocery stores operating in Chelsea and Lynn in Massachusetts, and in Providence, Rhode Island.

José Massó is a Latino radio host, civic leader, community activist, and educator. He has hosted and produced "¡Con Salsa!", a weekly music show on public radio, for 35 years in Boston. Massó currently serves as director of community relations for Massport.

Jacobo Negron is the president and founder of the Massachusetts Latino Police Officers Association.

Héctor Piña is local restaurateur and a leader in the Boston Latino community. Originally from the Dominican Republic, Piña owns two famed restaurants in Boston and is preparing to open a third.

Dan Rivera is the Mayor of Lawrence, the city with the largest share of Latino population in the state. Rivera is the only Latino mayor in Massachusetts.

State Representative **Jeffrey Sánchez** is the longest-serving Latino member in the Massachusetts legislature.

Francisco Ureña currently serves as Massachusetts Secretary of Veterans Affairs.

Miren Uriarte is a senior research associate at the Mauricio Gastón Institute for Latino Community Development and Public Policy in UMass Boston. In the early 90s, she served as the founding director of the institute, which was established by the Massachusetts state legislature to produce research on the growing Latino population in the state in order to better inform policymakers' decisions.

The **Vasallo Family** owns and operates the largest Latino newspaper in New England, El Mundo.

Social impact: nonprofits and how to get involved

The presence of universities and hospitals in Boston gives the region a strong nonprofit flavor — large, dominant institutions like MIT and Mass. General, Boston University and Children's Hospital, for example, cast a long shadow. But there's a whole other subset of the nonprofit world, the mission-oriented human services nonprofits that have evolved into one of the most creative and inspiring aspects of the Boston economy. Boston is a hotbed for innovative nonprofits dedicated to attacking societal problems in new ways.

Boston has thousands of nonprofits that target all kinds of social issues. There are over 34,000 nonprofits registered in Massachusetts, according to a 2012 report by the Boston Foundation, itself a nonprofit that helps donors target their charitable giving. Most nonprofits are local, grassroots organizations with small budgets and little or no staff. Above them, in terms of size, is a wide swath of social services, arts, and health care-related groups, an estimated 7,000 organizations that have revenue between $250,000 and $50 million, according to the Boston Foundation report.

> Even though they don't operate with profit motive, nonprofits are businesses all the same.

Even though they don't operate with profit motive, nonprofits are businesses all the same. They must sell themselves in the marketplace by competing for revenue, grants and donations; they have employees — the Museum of Science, for example, has over 430 of them. And if they fail to find support, they go out of business.

The vast array of nonprofits is difficult to categorize, so we'll pick a representative group of some of the largest, and then give you a sampling of relatively new, innovative nonprofits that have been started here and spread across the country.

Among the largest nonprofits (outside of higher education and health care), along with their 2015 annual revenue and employee count, from the Boston Business Journal, to give you a sense of their size:

The Museum of Fine Arts
Revenue: $151 million
Employees: 757
Mission: The region's preeminent museum

Mass. Audubon
Revenue: $29 million
Employees: 806
Mission: Runs nature sanctuaries across Massachusetts

MSPCA-Angell
Revenue: $61.8 million
Employees: 530
Mission: Boston's leading animal shelter and hospital

The Home for Little Wanderers
Revenue: $48 million
Employees: 705
Mission: Provides an array of services for children, including adoption, foster care, and residential care

Pine Street Inn
Revenue: $52 million
Employees: Over 500
Mission: A shelter for Boston's homeless and builder of permanent, affordable housing

Nonprofit boards: the critical factor for success

Nonprofits are thinly disguised businesses in many ways, but the most successful of them tend to have a secret weapon: Experienced, capable individuals who sit on the board of directors. These board members tend to come from the executive ranks of local business, and their expertise, guidance and capacity to raise funds help many nonprofits grow. A look at the boards of top area nonprofits shows how closely the for-profit and non-profit worlds are aligned. For example, the Boys and Girls Club of Boston, which serves 15,000 children and teens per year, has board members from top financial

institutions, including Jay Hooley, the CEO of State Street Corp. and Brian Moynihan, the CEO of Bank of America, on its board. Boards are never made up strictly of business leaders, for nonprofits benefit from having board members from all walks of life. Having high-level businesspeople to help solve problems and devise strategy often is a vital element.

Innovating in the nonprofit space

Just as there is a constant stream of startups in tech and biotech, there's been an abundance of nonprofit startups taking root in Boston. Social entrepreneurs, as they're called, have identified unmet needs and found new ways to deliver services. A good example of social innovation is a Boston-based nonprofit called Year Up, which was started by a successful tech entrepreneur named Gerald Chertavian who wanted to close the opportunity gap for urban young adults by providing six months of training in technical and professional skills, followed by another six months of on-the-job training through internships at participating companies. Year Up's innovation was to identify a vitally important mission — connecting potentially disenfranchised young adults to good opportunities, mostly in the entry-level tech and financial services space — and then execute a successful plan by finding financial and corporate support. No other nonprofit was doing this, nor were there effective government programs. The need for Year Up's services helped it rapidly expand across the country, to New York,

Among the many things for which Boston can take credit is this – it is a matter of pride for business leaders to support civic and charitable causes. Giving back is part of the DNA of the city. As you start your career, if you also pursue a passion for a cause or a charity, it will nourish your soul as well as expand your personal and professional network.

– Geri Denterlein, CEO and founder of Denterlein

Atlanta, Miami, Seattle, Philadelphia, Chicago and other cities. Year Up has a proven business model in tackling the "opportunity divide" while also providing much-needed, trained workers for employers.

Year Up is among several locally founded nonprofits that have spread to other cities. Here are a few others and what they do:

City Year, a nonprofit that partners with urban schools to place AmeriCorps members — people who commit for 10 months to working at the schools — to help students succeed. The program is now in 26 U.S. cities.

Cradles to Crayons has a mission to supply critically needed items for needy children. Volunteers stuff KidPacks with donated items, which are then donated through social services agencies. The nonprofit has opened a second location in Philadelphia.

Jumpstart connects college students and volunteers with preschool children to help them cultivate a love of language and learning. Jumpstart's idea of engaging young kids with the help of college students and others has spread across the country.

Citizen Schools partners with low-income middle schools to provide an expanded learning day with a range of learning opportunities by connecting the students with volunteers and other resources. Citizen Schools has expanded into six states outside of Massachusetts.

Social enterprise: New for-profit business models to address problems

One way to learn more about up-and-coming nonprofits is to attend the Social Innovation Showcase, an event organized by the Social Innovation Forum to help unique, effective nonprofits gain visibility and build a foundation for success. The Social Innovation Forum also focuses on the growing world of social enterprise — for-profit companies that have a mission to make the world a better place.

Susan Musinsky, the executive director of the Social Innovation Forum, says the influx of people with business skills to the nonprofit sector who a generation ago likely would gone into traditional business roles has helped accelerate innovation. Now there's something of a hybrid model emerging in the form of the social impact for-profit company. Their goal is to drive societal change with a sustainable business model.

"The conversation in the impact-investing space is, how to keep true to the values while creating a scalable product people will want to invest in," Musinsky said. And she predicts more money will gravitate toward social investing. "I think that, particularly, foundations whose goals are set up for philanthropic and societal benefit will begin to put more of their capital into investments that have social returns in the areas they're interested in."

Ideas to bring social change have become a bigger part of the startup scene, a trend that's on display at MassChallenge.

Ideas to bring social change have become a bigger part of the startup scene, a trend that's on display at MassChallenge, one of Boston's most prominent tech incubators. Of MassChallenge's 218 incubator companies in 2015, about 40 were categorized as "social impact" — for-profit companies with nonprofit missions.

To give you a flavor of some of the ideas, here are two finalists and their descriptions from the social impact category in the 2016 competition:

Joulez fuses arts and crafts with electronics to create fun and educational gadgets that inspire girls to get excited about STEM.

Solstice grows the market for clean energy by providing community-shared solar power to Americans that cannot install it on their own roof.

City Awake: Can Boston become the hub of social innovation?

Something spontaneous and remarkable happened at the end of 2014 when a new organization called City Awake created a social impact conference, putting a wide swath of nonprofits on display. City Awake saw an unmet need: A clearinghouse for sparking more civic awareness and engagement in Boston, especially with a new generation of Bostonians that is looking for opportunities to make a difference in the community. City Awake followed up with another successful expo in the fall of 2015.

City Awake, which was absorbed in the Greater Boston Chamber of Commerce as its civic innovation lab, touches on a powerful trend: A growing effort to harness the civic awareness and energy in Boston. One of the founders of City Awake, Justin Kang, told Boston.com in an interview in 2014 that he has grand ambitions for Boston. "Right now everyone wants to be the next tech center of the world," Kang said, now the executive director of the group. "In five years, everyone is going to want to be the purpose-driven city because that's what millennials are looking for."

OneIn3

The city of Boston has recognized an important demographic fact: One in three Bostonians is between the ages of 20-34, and this group will redefine the city in many ways. The city has formed a liaison office called OneIn3 Boston, and it is designed to help new Bostonians connect with resources and opportunities and its ONEin3 Council make recommendations to increase engagement of millennials with the city.

Some people to know in the nonprofit space:

Paul Grogan *(Bill Brett photo)*

Paul Grogan, CEO of the Boston Foundation. Well-known as a thought leader on Boston policy issues, Grogan also has been outspoken about the need to streamline the number of nonprofits in the region.

Matthew Teitelbaum is the new director of Boston's Museum of Fine Arts, taking over for longtime director Malcolm Rogers in mid-2015.

Justin Kang, City Awake cofounder and executive director, represents a new wave of thinking about how to activate more civic awareness in the next generation of Bostonians.

Justin Kang

Lynn Margherio, founder and CEO, Cradles to Crayons, has scaled the organization and pulled together powerful Boston and national boards of directors.

Vanessa Kirsch, president and founder of New Profit, a venture philanthropy fund, helps support innovative thinking in the nonprofit space.

Alan Khazei co-founded City Year and has since founded Be the Change (and is the husband of Vanessa Kirsch).

Michael Weekes, CEO of the Providers Council, leads a group that advocates for human services providers in Massachusetts.

John Fish *(Bill Brett photo)*

John Fish, the head of Suffolk Construction, and Jack Connors, founder of advertising firm Hill Holliday, are major forces in philanthropic circles, often playing leading roles in helping a variety of nonprofits raise money. Together they helped found a summer camp, Camp Harbor View, for inner-city youth.

International hub: 7 reasons why Boston is going global

The world increasingly is discovering Boston and Boston businesses increasingly are going global. In two areas the international trend is particularly strong: the lure of our colleges and universities for foreign students, and need for life sciences companies to be near our world-leading cluster of biotech and medical device firms.

Colleges and universities:

There are about 55,000 foreign-born graduate and undergraduate students in Massachusetts, a number that has increased rapidly in the past five years as local colleges have tapped into growing demand from Asia — especially China. At many local schools, the number of Chinese students has gone up over tenfold in the past five years, from a relative handful to in some cases thousands. The total numbers of foreign students in Massachusetts is up about 50 percent in the past five years.

Why are they coming to Boston? The city is seen as a sensible and safe destination to receive a coveted American degree.

According to the Institute of International Education, **here are the local universities with the highest numbers of foreign students:**

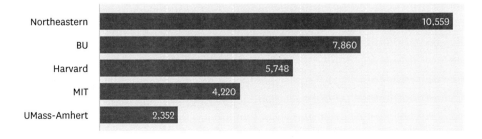

Northeastern: 10,559
BU: 7,860
Harvard: 5,748
MIT: 4,220
UMass-Amhert: 2,352

About 30 percent of the students are from China; students from India are a distant second at 11 percent.

Life sciences

Top biotech and pharmaceutical companies from around the globe have established U.S. headquarters here or acquired major local companies over the past 10 years. In the biggest acquisition, French pharma company Sanofi acquired Genzyme, one of Cambridge's most successful biotech pioneers.

Since the acquisition, which took place in 2011, Genzyme's workforce in Massachusetts has remained steady at about 5,000, and it has paid off for Sanofi, which is now embedded in the Massachusetts life sciences community. Another major entrant from abroad is Novartis, the Swiss pharmaceutical company, which moved its worldwide research headquarters to Cambridge in 2003. Now over 2,700 people work at its four-acre campus near MIT. Other international life sciences players include Japanese pharma company Takeda, which acquired Millennium in 2008; another Japanese pharma acquired Sepracor in 2010, changing its name to Sunovion. They employ over 500 people in Marlborough, Mass. AstraZeneca, a pharma firm based in London, has a significant beachhead in Cambridge, where 400 people work at its worldwide R&D center.

High-tech exports (and gold)

Massachusetts does manufacture a significant amount of tech hardware, scientific instrumentation and medical devices, which accounts for the bulk the state exports. Here's a chart from the U.S Census Bureau on Massachusetts export destinations:

But the reach of Massachusetts technology spans well beyond exports. Data storage firm EMC (which recently agreed to be acquired by Dell), which employs 60,000 and generates $25 billion in revenue, derives about 45 percent of its business outside of the U.S. Akamai, the Cambridge-based software company whose products speed up the Internet, does close to 30 percent of its business internationally.

In a funny quirk, Massachusetts' leading export is gold, odd for a place that has none underneath the ground. But some Massachusetts companies have established a niche as gold refiners, importing and then exporting gold to various countries.

Startups from Europe, Israel

The Boston area's fertile startup scene is a magnet for entrepreneurs, both from near and far. The region is particularly attractive for European and Israeli startups for three major reasons: The access to 1. talent 2. capital, and 3. the U.S. market. Boston's startup ecosystem, particularly its incubators like the Cambridge Innovation Center, offers support and advice to foreign startups looking to take root here. Young startups from abroad sometimes come with sponsorship funds from their governments to learn from other startups and business advisers. More mature startups are flocking here too, as one French entrepreneur told the Boston Business Journal in 2013, because Boston is considered the Silicon Valley of the East Coast, and it's geographically convenient for European companies.

Israel's strong culture of entrepreneurship has led to extensive cross-pollination in the Boston area economy. About 200 Massachusetts companies have Israeli connections, according to a report by the The New England-Israel Business Council. They employ 6,700 people in Massachusetts. One of the most prominent locally is CyberArk, a software security company with U.S. headquarters in Newton, Mass.

Residential and commercial real estate

Foreign investors are pouring money into Boston real estate, from skyscrapers to luxury condos. Foreign buyers spent $4.2 billion on Boston-area office properties in 2014, triple the total of the prior year. What's driving them to spend? They see Boston as a relative value to other cities, a stable economy with considerable upside in terms of rental rates. Another factor is Boston's historically difficult and expensive building environment. It takes time, money, and expertise to build in Boston, which has tended to limit supply and make existing properties, especially the most prominent of them, more desirable.

> **Thousands of new condos are being built in Boston, and a significant percentage of the buyers are foreign investors.**

Thousands of new condos are being built in Boston, and a significant percentage of the buyers are foreign investors.

Boston's booming luxury real estate market also has found an array of international buyers. Thousands of new condos are being built in Downtown Boston and the waterfront area in South Boston, and a significant percentage of the buyers are foreign investors who see Boston as one of a handful of top locations for residential real estate. The new wealth in China accounts for some of the buying, not only in the city but also in desirable suburban communities.

"To China's wealthiest investors, Boston looks like an underdeveloped growth market at bargain-basement prices," a recent Boston magazine story succinctly summarized the appeal of the city and region. According to the article, Boston is the 7th most appealing city in the world for real estate investment.

Asset management, banking

Boston's prestigious asset management industry has footholds all over the world, not only for business development but also as sources for labor. State Street Corp., for example, is a far-flung international corporation with offices in 29 countries, including a significant investment in Hangzhou, China, where it established a technology center — State Street Technology Zhejiang Co. — and employs over 1,000. Fidelity Investments has three major overseas centers, in Ireland, China and India, which provide a variety of support for Fidelity's operations.

Many foreign financial institutions have entered the Massachusetts market, often by acquisition. Banco Santander, one of Spain's largest banks, has a significant local presence after buying Sovereign Bank in 2009. Santander changed the Sovereign name in 2013 to expand its global brand. It employs 3,600 in Massachusetts. Several Canada financial institutions have large operations here, including John Hancock, a classic Boston brand that was acquired in 2004 by Manulife Financial. Sun Life Financial employs 1,600 in Wellesley, Mass. TD Bank, headquartered in Toronto, has 150 branches and over 1,700 employees in Massachusetts. And Citizens Bank, one of the largest banks in Massachusetts, was owned for years by the Royal Bank of Scotland until it was compelled to spin off Citizens in 2014 in order to generate cash to repay British taxpayers for bailing it out during the financial crisis of 2008-2009.

Tourist, business destination

As is evident by walking the streets of the city, tourists flock to Boston from near and far. Tourists come for the mix of history, charm and amenities (the shopping and dining) that the region offers. Massachusetts had 1.79 million overseas visitors in 2015, according to information supplied by the Greater Boston Convention and Visitors Bureau. Roughly 75 percent of the visitors were tourists (rather than business travelers). About 50 percent of the visitors come from Europe. About 25 percent come from Asia.

Boston ranked 10th in North America for international overnight visitors in 2014. When factoring in domestic and Canadian visitors to the greater Boston region, Boston had 19.1 million visitors. More tourism and visitor data, international and otherwise, is available on the GBCVB website.

Rich Boston, poor Boston — the income gap and what can be done about it

Thomas Leighton

He owns only 2 percent of the company. Yet this small fraction is worth $250 million.

He is Akamai CEO and co-founder Thomas Leighton, the MIT professor who led a team of graduate students to create algorithms to speed up the Internet. Leighton's brilliance and good fortune as an Internet pioneer is a classic example of a phenomenon that's making Massachusetts CEOs richer than ever.

But look a little closer, and you'll find that it's not only the very top crust that is getting wealthy.

That's because for every Leighton there are thousands of stock market winners in Massachusetts. These are relatively ordinary folks who have their own tiny fractions of their companies' stock shares and now are sitting on a pile of valuable equity. It is not simply that the top dog takes all, as much as it may seem like it as we read about one outsized annual pay package after another. As Boston reaches maturity as a leading innovator in many sectors, those ownership gains are reaching deeper into the workforce.

These are the winners. The issue is the proverbial rising tide doesn't lift all boats. As worry grows about the widening income inequality, Massachusetts' economy is emblematic of the trends that are driving the divide. A recent report by the Brookings Institution ranks Boston third in the country for the highest ratio between the average household income of the top 5 percent of earners ($239,900) and the bottom 20 percent ($15,900).

The Boston area is among the best places in the world to grow rich, and one of the hardest places to be poor.

This prolonged wealth accumulation, partly the result of the stock market rising by over 60 percent in the past five years along with a slew of new, public companies with soaring share prices, is a product of companies sharing the upside with various levels of employees through stock options and stock grants.

Boston's wealth accumulation is modest compared to Silicon Valley, where stock market wealth has created legions of millionaires and bungalows that sell for $1 million.

One lesson to be gleaned from the equity explosion is that ownership is critical for wealth accumulation, and in an economy like Boston's, stock options and grants can bring outsized gains.

The question should not be how do we stop or punish this phenomenon, even though it's startling how a new class of quasi-lottery winners are cashing in. It's how do we draw in more mini-owners and spread the wealth further.

The new wealthy are not necessarily high-net-worth individuals. Many are fairly average people, often mid-level employees whose company's stock has slowly and steadily appreciated, or like in the case of Biogen, taken off like a rocket ship. Usually it's not enough money to allow them to retire, but it can be life-changing all the same. A researcher at Biogen, for example, who received 2,000 stock options five years ago, and another 1,000 shares in bonuses over the next two years would be sitting on close to $750,000 in vested stock.

But it's not just Biogen, whose stock price has tripled in the past five years. Companies like Thermo Fisher, and Skyworks Solutions aren't exactly household names like Facebook and Twitter, but each brings in over $1 billion in revenue and has at least tripled its stock price in the past three years. The internal "owners" of these companies, and ones that have enjoyed similar success, like Vertex, State Street Corp., and TJX, are doing quite well. Add in relatively new public companies, high flyers like athenahealtha and TripAdvisor, companies that each employ well over 1,000, and the picture forms of a new wave of employee-owners, in some many cases mini-millionaires.

The amount of equity that companies share with employees varies widely, depending on the stage of the company and its industry. The National Center for Employee Ownership estimates that employees control about 8 percent of corporate equity. That number, however, includes private, employee-owned companies, and the percentage of public company equity held by employees is likely much lower.

In an economy like Boston's, stock options and grants can bring outsized gains.

All the same, startups and established public companies generally give equity awards to most employees, even if it's small amounts.

In biotech, it's routine to give almost every employee a tiny stake in the company when they start, followed by annual awards of stock options and restricted stock, depending on performance. This doesn't make millionaires out of many rank-and-file employees, but it can pay off college tuition or home loans.

While the broader public may be aghast at CEO pay, when these executives are winning, so too are a wide swath of employees. CEO compensation, while consistently exorbitant, usually is a proxy for more modest wealth accumulation inside the company.

Not everyone wins the stock option game, of course. Many employees receive stock options that end up worthless, as their company's share price swoons below the strike price that would put the options in the money.

And the market may fall and crater many fortunes that are tethered to company stock. It has happened before and it will happen again.

Meanwhile, a broad swath of Bostonians can only imagine the opportunities many of these growth companies offer. They are blocked out by many factors, but none more than a lack of educational and training opportunities. The new economy surges ahead, demanding sets of skills that are harder for those in lower income levels to obtain. Thus, the gap between rich and poor, given the trends in the Boston economy, is destined to widen unless there's a concerted effort to ramp up the connections between Boston's leading companies and the people who need the jobs most.

Highest paid Boston-area executives 2015

1	Hari Ravichandran	$35,995,658	Endurance International
2	Jeffrey Leiden	$28,099,826	Vertex Pharmaceuticals
3	Ernie Herrman	$20,020,652	The TJX Cos. Inc.
4	Carol Meyrowitz	$17,962,232	The TJX Cos.
5	Sean Healey	$17,506,689	Affiliated Managers Group
6	George Scangos	$16,689,662	Biogen Inc.
7	Marc Casper	$16,307,079	Thermo Fisher Scientific
8	Jeremy Delinsky	$13,834,644	Wayfair Inc.
9	Thomas Kennedy	$12,796,608	Raytheon Co.
10	Laurence James Neil Cooper	$12,465,359	Ziopharm Oncology Inc.

Source: Boston Business Journal

One of the economic ironies in Massachusetts is the vast number of unfilled jobs — largely open because of a lack of qualified people — and the hundreds of thousands of people in the state who can't find work. Closing this skills gap is the crucial public policy challenge in truly addressing the income gap.

Housing, high costs, and the prospects for growth: A Mass. policy primer

There's a price Massachusetts pays for its economic success: higher costs, both for individuals and businesses. Boston is among the most expensive places to live in the country. The Hub recently ranked 3rd in a Forbes survey of the "Most Overpriced Cities." In every cost category — housing, health care, transportation, food, utilities — Boston was significantly above the national average.

The Boston area traditionally has not produced enough housing to keep up with demand, the most obvious reason for its high housing costs. Greater Boston housing starts are limited by the population density, the high cost of land, and restrictive zoning. Massachusetts cities and towns issued building permits for about 14,500 units in 2014; for context, North Carolina produced nearly 50,000 units in 2014, or three times the number for a population that's only 50 percent larger. Much of the new housing that's being built in Boston is high-priced, in part because it's more difficult and less profitable to build anything else. As buying a home becomes more elusive for those with average incomes and rents continue to rise rapidly, one looming policy question is what can be done to create more reasonably priced housing.

One looming policy question is what can be done to create more reasonably priced housing.

The creation of additional supply is critical. Boston Mayor Marty Walsh, recognizing the effect of housing costs on the fabric of the city, has launched an ambitious plan to build 53,000 units for all income levels by 2030. Accelerating housing production — beyond the already considerable quantity of luxury housing underway — will require zoning changes to allow more density, as well as tax breaks for developers who build for middle-income and lower-income residents.

Transportation: a bumpy road

New housing creation is closely linked to public transportation, another cause for concern. As the winter of 2015 definitively proved, much of Greater Boston's transportation infrastructure is antiquated and neglected. It is not anyone's idea of a 21st Century transportation system. Transportation officials pegged the backlog of "state of good repair" items for the Massachusetts Bay Transportation Authority (MBTA) at $7.3 billion. The MBTA runs on a budget that's slightly under $2 billion annually. Turning around the reliability of the public transportation system is a priority for Gov. Charlie Baker, who took office in January 2015. Efforts to address the longstanding neglect of roads and bridges also are underway. In short, the region's first-class economy is not adequately supported by its transportation system, another clear risk to future growth. Fixing the T and addressing infrastructure needs have suddenly emerged as top policy issues as the shortcomings of the region's transportation system have become a political hot-button issue.

Health care and electricity rates

The finest health care system in the country also generates among the highest costs. Massachusetts ranks third in the country for the total premium cost of individual coverage — 9 percent higher than the national average and 13 percent higher than North Carolina, according to a recent report by the Massachusetts Taxpayers Foundation. Among the reasons: Massachusetts patients tend to receive care at more expensive academic institutions and the state has been slower to adopt consumer-driven health plans with lower costs and higher deductibles.

Electricity: Massachusetts ranks 3rd highest in the country for electricity costs, behind Hawaii and Alaska. Electricity costs for industrial and commercial users also are among the highest in the country — Massachusetts' industrial electricity rates are 93 percent above the national average. Much of the higher costs are attributed to the volatility of natural gas prices and the limitations on the pipelines that supply Massachusetts power plants. The higher costs put large energy users — for example, manufacturers — at a competitive disadvantage.

How to best grow the Massachusetts economy?

Exporting some of Boston's success: While the greater Boston economy is thriving, it abuts other Massachusetts subeconomies that aren't doing nearly as well. One of the challenges and great opportunities for the state is to export its success to other regions of the state, especially old, industrial cities that need more jobs. Cities like Lawrence, Fitchburg, Holyoke, and Springfield, among the so-called "Gateway Cities," have great potential if they can be better connected to the economic activity in Boston.

Education and job training: Massachusetts' August 2015 unemployment rate was 4.7 percent, meaning about 170,000 residents were unemployed. Around the same time, there were 107,000 Massachusetts jobs listed on Indeed.com alone. There's no question that the potential growth of Boston economy is threatened by the need for more skilled workers. In the manufacturing sector alone, the aging of the workforce is expected to create some 100,000 openings by 2022, according to a report by Northeastern economist Barry Bluestone (published in 2012). Addressing the skills gap to bring more underemployed and unemployed people into higher paid jobs would grow the number of jobs in the state and improve the quality of life for many. That's why there's a strong emphasis on science, technology, engineering and math (STEM) coursework from grade school to graduate school in Massachusetts. That's where the jobs are heading, and yet students' overall competency in these areas isn't rising to keep up with the expected needs of the next-generation economy.

Massachusetts patients tend to receive care at more expensive academic institutions, driving up health care costs.

"We really need to focus on the middle class and the skills gap," said Suffolk Construction President and CEO John Fish, a longtime leader of two major business groups — the Greater Boston Chamber of Commerce and the Massachusetts Competitive Partnership. "I think we have to reengineer our community colleges and some of the state colleges. Are those community colleges responding to the job needs in that area? We need to think about where the puck is going, not where it is now. They should be sitting down and working with business and government and defining what those needs are going to be."

Expanding Massachusetts' top talent clusters: Despite the impressive amount of talent in technology and science that drives the regional economy, the human capital needs of its high-tech and biotech companies already can't

Why visa reform, STEM education is critical for the Massachusetts economy

"Our economy is growing but the areas where we are seeing growth are areas where highly skilled workers in the STEM fields are needed to fill open positions—IT, life sciences, engineering, advanced manufacturing. Unfortunately, we simply do not have the type of trained workforce availably to keep up with growth in these areas. There are two things we need to do to fix this. First, we need to update our immigration system, specifically as it relates to H-1B visas. We need to increase the cap on those

Jim Brett *(Photo by John Gillooly)*

visas so that when international students graduate from our top-notch colleges and universities, they can remain here in the U.S. and fill some of these positions, rather than returning home to work for our overseas competition. Second, we need to invest in STEM education, and at a very early age. We must develop a domestic pipeline of highly skilled workers in the STEM fields and the only way to do that is to start early and get kids excited about math and science and careers in fields like information technology, life sciences, and advanced manufacturing."

— Jim Brett, CEO, The New England Council

be filled. The demand likely will grow significantly over the next decade, especially in fields like cybersecurity and data management. Some business leaders believe Boston should leverage the power of its higher education institutions and leading companies to create a broader pool of talent. Two Boston financial services CEOs, Robert Reynolds of Putnam Investments and Clayton Deutsch of Boston Private Financial Holdings, said in a recent Boston Globe op-ed that their industry needs to think ahead to stay ahead in cultivating new talent: "Boston has a distinct advantage in cultivating the talent that could sustain — or increase — its role as a financial services hub, but it needs greater public-private collaboration to leverage the many assets already in place."

Competition and the role of economic development institutions

Massachusetts competes with other states for jobs. The contest often starts when a local company considers its expansion options — and other states, either directly or indirectly may offer compelling business advantages, such as tax breaks or a more abundant workforce. Officials and business leaders increasingly have recognized the potential of investing resources into cultivating some of Massachusetts' economic advantages and addressing some of its shortcomings. The state's **Office of Housing and Economic Development** focuses on many economic priorities, including facilitating job growth by working with companies that wish to expand or may consider expanding or relocating to Massachusetts. In a state with no shortage of regulations, state government realizes it needs to be a liaison for businesses looking to navigate bureaucracy. Other states often succeed in making permitting faster and more predictable than Massachusetts.

Massachusetts has several other agencies that help facilitate business expansion. Among them:

MassDevelopment helps finance and manage development projects, including affordable housing and industrial sites. In its 2014 fiscal year, it financed or developed more than 300 projects.

Mass Tech Collaborative is a government-funded entity that focuses on the tech economy, charged with creating collaborations between government, business and higher education. Among its projects, it runs the Innovation Institute and the MassTech Intern Partnership.

MassEcon is a private sector partner helping companies expand or relocate. It holds an annual Team Massachusetts Economic Impact Awards luncheon that celebrates company expansion and investment.

In the battle for policies to push for economic growth, one thought leader is the Pioneer Institute, a free-market-oriented think tank that is a strong supporter of charter schools and has advocated for reforms to improve public transportation, among other causes. Pioneer, which believes government should innovate, is led by executive director Jim Stergios.

Politicians, policy-makers to the rescue

Although Massachusetts is an overwhelmingly Democratic state, its recently elected governor, Charlie Baker, is a Republican. Baker won in part because he successfully appealed to Massachusetts' independent voters — those not registered with either party. Independents make up 53 percent of the state's registered voters (Democrats have 36 percent and Republicans, 11 percent). Massachusetts, despite being the home state to liberal leaders like Elizabeth

Warren and Barney Frank, is not as left-leaning as it may seem. Here are some of the top politicians and policy-makers in the state:

Gov. Charlie Baker

Gov. Charlie Baker took office in January 2015, bringing a combination of government and private sector experience. Baker was the CEO of health care insurer Harvard Pilgrim before making an unsuccessful bid for governor in 2010. Among Baker's priorities are upgrading public transportation service and expanding economic opportunity across the entire state and addressing the Massachusetts opioid epidemic.

Sen. Elizabeth Warren is considered one of the most powerful liberal politicians in the country, winning a loyal following for her consumer advocacy work and willingness to take on large financial institutions. Her Massachusetts colleague in the Senate is **Ed Markey**, a longtime congressman who won election to the Senate in 2013.

Boston Mayor Marty Walsh took office in January 2014. One of his immediate priorities was to make Boston more responsive to younger Bostonians' desire to expand the hours of the city's night life to 4 a.m.

Jay Ash and **Stephanie Pollack** are two key members of Gov. Baker's administration. Ash is the secretary of the Office of Housing and Economic Development and is point person for implementing policies to grow the Massachusetts economy. Pollack is the Secretary of the Massachusetts Department of Transportation and responsible for shoring up the Commonwealth's public transportation service

Two most powerful people at the State House, aside from Gov. Baker, are **Speaker of the House Robert DeLeo** and **Senate President Stanley Rosenberg**, both Democrats with considerable leverage to help shape economic policy.

PART FOUR

The Boston job hunt — lessons, data and resources

How to stand out from the crowd: What hiring executives are looking for

If you're a soon-to-be college graduate looking to kick-start your career in Greater Boston, timing is certainly on your side. The city's economy remains strong as a lot of companies are ramping up their recruitment for fresh talent. The question for those looking to enter the job market is: How to find what you're looking for, and when you do, make sure you're not lost in the shuffle.

That's because landing a job, even entry-level positions here, remains competitive. For every Boston-area job you apply for that's posted on Monster, Indeed and LinkedIn, you'll likely be going up against hundreds of other candidates who are just as qualified as you are — or at least pretending to be.

According to human resource professionals who understand the Boston job market better than anyone, it's all about obtaining some of the skills you'll need while still in college, and then taking the time to find and target the companies that align with your career goals.

Tracy Burns

Anyone on the hiring side of things will also tell you that it takes a lot of smart networking and then being able to differentiate yourself from other candidates.

"It takes a lot of work to find a good job," said Tracy Burns, the chief executive officer for Northeast Human Resources Association (NEHRA). "You really have to approach it like a full-time job."

Burns said that while the best practices for finding a job haven't changed that much over the last 20 years, technology, for better or worse, has had a huge impact on the entire process. But there's no substitute for old-fashioned networking – only now technology enables job candidates to more quickly expand their networks.

"The biggest trend in HR has been the use of the Internet and social media. It has helped speed up the process on both ends considerably," she said. "Finding job opportunities and information about companies is at your fingertips now. Job seekers can apply for (with just a few clicks on the computer) and hiring managers can screen literally hundreds of resumes in a matter of seconds."

All the advanced technology isn't a panacea, however. "Almost all the larger companies are using applicant tracking systems that do key word searches for them," Burns said. "Because of that, applicants really need to customized their resumes for each specific job using the job descriptions as their guide."

Burns cautions all job searchers that hiring managers can access personal information about anyone on the Internet now. Along with your resume and LinkedIn profiles, companies are searching popular social media sites such as Facebook and Instagram and now Snapchat for insight into your personal lives.

"When you're on the hiring side and evaluating talent, you don't want to hire someone who shows bad judgment on social media, " Burns said. "Once it's on the Internet it doesn't go away. It's permanent."

Understanding how companies are screening and evaluating job candidates today is just the first step in breaking into the Boston job market. The next step is how to construct an effective resume and a LinkedIn profile that stands out from the crowd, according to Lauri Rich, the director of outreach and career development for Boston University's School of Public Health.

Building your brand

"Your resume is your value proposition. It is your brand and so you need to highlight your highest level of accomplishment at everything you've done up until then," said Rich, who has over 30 years of experience on the hiring side. "My philosophy on resumes is that it should emphasize results and outcomes, versus tasks and responsibilities."

Michael Dean, the senior vice president and head of human resources for Harvard Management Company, Inc., warns that even one mistake on a resume, no matter how small it might be, is always going to be a game ender for him when evaluating talent.

"Your resume has to be perfect. It's a reflection of you. It's your marketing plan," he said.

Dean said he looks for a record of achievement on resumes, along with clues to a well-rounded person who has the ability to learn and work hard.

"I also want to know that they can communicate effectively and problem solve in a collaborative workplace. You usually don't learn that until you bring them in for interviews," he said.

Preparing for the interview

In a career that has spanned over 40 years and includes executive positions at Fortune 500 companies, Dean said he has hired hundreds of college graduates. And while he's impressed with how technologically savvy and career driven today's young professionals are, he's often taken aback by how little candidates prepare themselves for interviews, whether they be by phone or face-to-face.

> "I want to know pretty quickly that they did their research and understand our company and who our competition is."
> —Michael Dean

"I'm always amazed when I talk to a recent graduate and it becomes real obvious," he said about poorly prepared candidates. "I want to know pretty quickly that they did their research and understand our company and who our competition is."

Dean said that all soon-to-be college graduates should be asking themselves the following questions — before even beginning their job search:

- What am I consuming? In other words, what am I reading, listening to and watching to better inform you about what is happening in the marketplace?

- Who am I spending time with and building networks and contacts that can help me in my career search?

- Who are my role models? Have I developed any career mentors? Who can help me open doors?

Dean said it's imperative that any job searcher, especially college students, develop a project plan for his/her career — with goals, time lines, deliverables, metrics for success, etc. — that are clearly identified and, most importantly, achievable.

One thing, Dean, Burns and Rich all agree on is that a job search takes time and effort. They caution anyone trying to enter the workforce for the first time not to be overconfident and feel they are entitled to their dream job right out of school.

"Students are much more savvy now, more advanced, no doubt about it," Rich said. "They also have a very high level of expectation about their careers. A lot of them go into the job-searching process thinking 'I should get this job.' They don't want to believe they are not going to get the job they want.

"It's still very much a competitive job market out there, so no one should be surprised if they don't get their first choice," Rich said.

Adventures in finding the right job:
Lessons from recent Boston graduates

Tim Katz hoped to be a high school teacher and ended up training employees at a Boston-area nonprofit organization. Britt Dresser envisioned becoming a newspaper sports writer and ended up working on the business side at a prominent TV and magazine company in Boston.

The two recent college grads, and thousands of others like them in Greater Boston, were liberal arts majors, uncertain of their career prospects after school. Unlike other college grads, such as engineering majors, their degrees weren't in red-hot professional fields that ensured them plenty of high-paying job offers soon after college.

> "Even if you're struggling to find exactly what you want, you need to spin your experience and skills in the general direction you want."
>
> — Britt Dresser

For liberal arts majors, there is usually no easy, straight path from getting a diploma to landing their first paycheck. And finding the right job, even if you're in a high-demand field like accounting or computer science, isn't simple either.

And while twists and turns, false starts and rejections often are inevitable, the point of *The Boston Economy — Understanding and Accessing One of the World's Greatest Job Markets* is to help emerging students and recent grads gain a broader sense of what's available to them. Once you broaden the possibilities, then you can create networks to access them.

Networks matter, for sure, and so do internships. But as these profiles of job hunters show, perseverance is an important ingredient to success. The newly minted graduates profiled in this chapter initially followed their general interests, stayed determined and flexible despite setbacks, and ultimately parlayed the skills they gained into jobs with similar traits to what they originally sought.

They also took full advantage of Greater Boston's diverse economy, learning from early job-search failures and usually tapping into networks of friends, relatives, former students and even mere acquaintances working in the deep and rich array of private- and public-sector institutions in the Boston region.

"Even if you're struggling to find exactly what you want, you need to spin your experience and skills in the general direction you want," advises Dresser, an Emerson College grad with a journalism degree. "You have to keep trying."

Following are some brief stories — and career-search lessons — from a number of recent grads who have found jobs in Greater Boston, usually after many twists and turns after leaving campus:

Tim Katz, University of Massachusetts-Amherst, 2013; majors in history and legal studies: After graduating from UMass, Katz initially followed his dream to be a high school teacher by joining Teach for America, a nonprofit organization helping with the education needs of students from lower-income families.

After a year teaching social studies to middle-school students in Memphis, Tenn., Katz returned to the Boston area with the goal of landing a high school teaching job. Though he got a teaching license, it was still hard to land a position without a master's degree.

"I was very discouraged," Katz said of the lackluster response from schools he applied to.

To earn money and pay the bills, he eventually applied and interviewed for sales jobs at an insurance company, a roofing and remodeling firm and other entities in the Boston area. And he also applied for a non-licensed medical assistant job at Planned Parenthood, the nonprofit women's health group.

During the interview process, officials at Planned Parenthood noticed Katz's teaching experience and his skills at developing curriculum materials — and he was offered a job helping to train new workers at Planned Parenthood in Worcester.

"I am absolutely still teaching," said Katz of his post as a non-licensed medical assistant in charge of employee training. "I like the job a lot. It's opened up my options. In the future, I can see applying this to training positions at schools or at other jobs."

Lessons learned and advice from Katz: Be persistent and don't get discouraged; network with as many people and as early as possible; value and market the skills you've gained, and always be flexible.

Britt Dresser, Emerson College, 2009, major in print journalism: It certainly wasn't a straight shot from college to America's Test Kitchen for Britt Dresser.

Britt Dresser

After leaving Emerson, Dresser found it hard to crack into the journalism field as a sports writer (specifically as a baseball writer). She had done some sports-writing internships at daily newspapers during college and "later applied for every full-time journalism job I could find."

But the only full-time newspaper jobs available were for general-assignment reporting positions, not sports writing jobs, and they were all low paying. A native of the Detroit area, Dresser ended up at the Lynn Item and later worked at local chain of newspapers covering the town of Beverly and the Cape Ann area, north of Boston.

The long hours, low pay and lack of sports-writing opportunities ultimately discouraged her from pursuing her chosen career path as a sports writer. "It was hard," she said. "I realized I couldn't do writing the way I wanted to do it. I was worn down."

Reluctantly, she left journalism for a better-paying web production job at a local research company, but she was also out of the media world.

Yet she later heard from a college friend about a job opening at America's Test Kitchen, a unit of Boston Common Press, the producer of the popular Public Broadcasting Corporation cooking show of the same name and publisher of the cooking magazine Cook's Illustrated. Her friend knew she might be interested working at a media company again — and he was right.

She ultimately landed a job as a project manager, coordinating book and magazine deadlines with vendors. In other words, it was a job on the business side of the media industry, not the editorial side, but Dresser said she's happy. "It's a lot of pressure, but it's a good type of pressure," she said.

Dresser may not be perched high up in a stadium press box keeping tabs on unfolding baseball games below, but she is in the thick of the media world with a full-time job, benefits and "working with really smart people."

"My varied background really helped in getting the job," she said.

Lessons learned and advice from Dresser: Keep friends and others informed about your interests and goals, and gain skills that can be applied to future jobs you may not even be aware of at the time.

Emily Mulloy

Emily Mulloy, Boston University, 2013; majors in psychology and international relations: A native of Wisconsin, Mulloy wanted to remain in Boston after college to take advantage of local connections and the diverse industries in the area, but it wasn't easy.

Before graduation, she had interned in a charitable organization's human resources department and found she really liked the field. The interaction with current and potential employees dovetailed with her interests in psychology — and so her job search started with her targeting human-resource opportunities.

She interviewed with a global consulting firm in Boston and even an area tech firm — but didn't get the jobs. "I was very disappointed and depressed," she said.

But using LinkedIn and other online career sites, she noticed an HR opening at Forrester Research in Boston. Besides thoroughly researching the company, she recalled that the tech-company executive she had previously interviewed with had urged her to stay in touch. So she took him up on the offer, contacted him and found out that he actually knew someone at Forrester — and he made a call on her behalf.

She ended up getting the HR associate job. She said she's glad she stuck with her strategy of focusing her jobs search on Boston, where she had built a strong network of connections. "It's a great city for those starting their careers."

Lessons learned and advice from Mulloy: Start networking in college and stay in touch with people, even acquaintances who casually offer to help in a job search; also, research companies thoroughly before job interviews.

James Doherty, Stonehill College, 2012; major in political science: Not everyone goes through a tortuous job-search process soon after college graduation. Sometimes the tough decisions are made before graduation — with positive results.

In the case of James Doherty, who majored in political science and minored in philosophy at Stonehill College, he envisioned going to law school and possibly entering politics after school. He had even taken the LSATs in preparation of pursuing a legal career.

While still at Stonehill, he also did an internship with the Massachusetts Democratic State Party, recruiting college students for campaign work and other volunteer functions. He interviewed dozens of students, reviewed their resumes and assessed their qualifications.

"I enjoyed it a lot," he said of his management-like experience.

The job-clincher for Doherty: He already had experience interviewing job candidates and screening applicants as a result of his internship.

In the spring of his senior year in 2012, he attended a campus job fair, though not with much optimism. "I didn't think I'd find a job. But a friend told me about a recruitment company at the fair called WinterWyman. Truthfully, I didn't know what WinterWyman did."

So at the fair, he met with representatives from the Waltham company, gave them his resume and was briefly interviewed. A few weeks later, he was brought in for another interview at WinterWyman's offices. Afterward, he went out of his way to convey to WinterWyman he was very interested in working at the company.

Before he graduated that spring, he had a job offer in hand as a senior account manager who helps all types of companies find qualified contract workers. The clincher in Doherty's favor: He already had experience interviewing job candidates and screening applicants as a result of his internship.

"I liked interviewing and listening to people's stories," he said of the skills he gained in college. "I liked fitting people's skills to jobs."

Ultimately, that's exactly what officials at WinterWyman did with Doherty's skills: They fit them to a full-time job.

Lessons learned and advice from Doherty: Start a job search while still in college, do internships, attend job fairs, remain flexible about job opportunities and "show companies that you really want the job."

Bethany Burns, Suffolk University, 2012; major in fine arts and interior design: Bethany Burns knew what she wanted to do after college and eventually got what she wanted. But it was still a very bumpy, frustrating experience to get from here to there, so to speak.

A fine arts and interior design major at Suffolk University, Burns was lucky to have two internships during college, both of them at design firms in Boston. She continued with one of the internships for a few months after graduation because she didn't have a full-time job offer.

She ultimately cut the internship cord in August 2012 so she could commit as much time as possible to her job search. A native of Rhode Island, she focused her search on the Boston and Rhode Island markets, actually considered by many professionals to be the same eastern New England market in general.

She said she applied to 15 to 20 design firms, half of whom didn't even respond. Some merely emailed rejected notices. With large student-loan payments due, she started getting nervous. "It was pretty frustrating, but I was still hopeful."

In the fall of 2012, she landed a job with a small residential architectural design firm in Boston's Back Bay, J. Schwartz Design, and she later used the experience she gained there to win a job at LLB Architects in Pawtucket, R.I., nearer to her native home.

Lessons learned and advice from Burns: Take internships seriously, start developing networks and nearby connections in college, research companies you're applying to, and "always be persistent and don't give up."

New options and best practices for landing an internship

There is no shortage of internship-related websites that are populated with potential opportunities for would-be interns. A visit to mega-jobsites like Simplyhired.com can quickly create a sorted local list of companies in search of interns. There also are more targeted sites, like Internships.com and Looksharp.com. Surprisingly, many of them stipulate they don't pay, which is definitely a no-no with federal authorities, especially if students don't receive college credit for the experience.

Despite the seeming abundance of internship opportunities, there remains a disconnect between businesses and aspiring students. The supply of interns oftentimes is not meeting demand, and the hodge-podge of online listings is an inefficient way for companies and students to find one another. Finding a good internship, like any successful endeavor, involves some planning, hard work, and persistence.

Best practices for finding an internship

» Personal networking generally is far more effective in landing an internship than the jobsites. Why? It's easy to get lost in the shuffle online. You may be perfect for the internship, but the volume of applicants may mean your resume won't receive proper scrutiny. Don't get us wrong: the job boards and internship-specific websites like Internship.com can be very useful, and you should use them. But your odds of landing an internship are much higher through a connection who knows you and wants to help you.

» Timing is everything — make sure you're applying during the proper window. Many students start their internship search too late. For example, if you're looking for a summer internship, it's wise to begin your queries right after the New Year, if not earlier. Sometimes with internships, it's first-come, first-served.

» Talk to classmates about their experiences. They're often the best sources for targeting good internships, and they can help you avoid ones that may not be the right fit. Also, when you talk with classmates about their internships, make sure to get names and contact info of the people who supervised them.

» Tap into your school's alumni network. Alumni generally go the extra mile for undergrads at their alma mater. It's their way of giving back. LinkedIn is a good tool to tap into alums from your school. Don't be shy about asking for favors and advice from alums about internships.

» Deploy the resources of your school's career services. This may seem obvious, but too many students don't make the most of their schools' in-house resources. Staff there may have some internship ideas you never considered.

» Don't be afraid to use the side door to get an internship. Target the decision-makers (even the CEO, depending on the size of the company), and not only the resume screeners, when applying. It's sometimes effective to avoid bureaucracy and instead approach those who actually have the hiring power.

» Tenacity counts. Most businesspeople are very busy and sometimes don't respond to emails very quickly — or at all, unless you send a follow-up reminder. There's a fine line between being persistent and being a pest — but two or three follow-up emails or calls is reasonable.

» Customize your resume for the opportunity at hand. If you use the one-resume-fits-all approach, you may be selling yourself short. In customizing your resume, emphasize practical work experience and personal initiative. Companies want interns to be self-starters. They're not nearly as interested in your academic accomplishments as your real-world experience.

» Do your homework on the company — before you apply for the internship, and, of course, when you have the interview.

» In the interview, be prepared to ask as many questions as you're asked. It's a mistake to be passive and allow the interview to become an interrogation. The interview should be a conversation, and your curiosity about the company — its competitive position, its corporate culture, and how you can best make a contribution — is critical in making a good impression. And make sure you follow up quickly with a thank-you note. In the world of constant electronic communication, an old-fashioned, handwritten note will help you be remembered.

The need to make better connections for interns has led Boston-area companies and business groups to get better organized in culling together and promoting internship opportunities. There are new resources, including some websites that are funded by state government, that gather internship opportunities in one place.

Websites aggregating opportunities for internships, from big data, startups and beyond, are growing.

The Mass Tech Collaborative runs a state-funded internship program for students interested in tech-oriented companies (although the MTC website says the funding has expired). All the same, there's a sign-in process that puts student candidates in a pool for variety of internships. masstech.org/intern

For students looking to zero in on big data internship opportunities, the Mass Tech Collaborative also hosts a website dedicated to big data, including a Big Data job board, a meta-listing of opportunities. It includes an option to search for big data-related internships. massbigdata.org/jobs

The New England Venture Capital Association has launched a website to connect students with the startup scene. Called Tech Generation, thetechgeneration.com the website already boasts over 90 participating companies and has enrolled more than 300 would-be interns and plans to run a year-round program.

Internship outreach extends beyond strictly tech. The Greater Boston Chamber of Commerce, in partnership with the Boston Federal Reserve Bank, has launched The Internship Collaborative, an initiative to connect students with area employers. When last checked in October of 2015, this website, Intern Hub, had over 1,100 listings. internhub.internships.com/join

One shouldn't ignore possibilities in state and local government. The City of Boston, an employer of over 17,000, features internship opportunities on this web page: cityofboston.gov/internships Likewise, the Commonwealth of Massachusetts offers internships in its many branches. For example, the State Treasurer's office has a year-round program with application instructions on this web page: mass.gov/treasury/about/employment-and-internships/internships.html

Boston's many business groups

There is no single voice of business in Boston because the Boston business community is really an assortment of many different communities with different priorities. As such, the Boston area does not lack for business groups. One group represents the interests of big business while another caters exclusively to the needs of small business. There are a variety of trade groups — in retail, biotech, advertising, technology and accounting, among others.

One thing they all have in common is they create fertile opportunities for networking. There is no better way to experience a cross section of the Boston economy than by attending a business group event. Emerging students seeking a spot in the Boston economy should keep in mind that there's a strong benefit in presenting oneself in person. Business groups and gatherings provide ample opportunity to meet decision-makers, or people who can connect you to hiring managers. Below are brief descriptions of the Boston area's top business groups.

Greater Boston Chamber of Commerce: The most prominent of Boston's business groups, the Greater Boston Chamber has a new leader — President and CEO James Rooney, the former head of the Massachusetts Convention Center Authority. The chamber is a large organization with members from every conceivable industry, and it specializes in bringing top business and political leaders before its membership. The chamber's annual meeting in May draws close to 2,000 people.

Associated Industries of Massachusetts: AIM is a statewide organization that serves all of Massachusetts. No business group has more of an impact on business public policy than AIM, which focuses on regulatory and business-cost issues. Led by president and CEO Rick Lord, the group celebrated its 100th anniversary in the fall of 2015.

National Federation of Independent Business — Massachusetts: NFIB is dedicated to serving small businesses and advocates for policies that hit small businesses the hardest, including health care and taxation. Bill Vernon, a former legislator, leads the group.

Massachusetts Competitive Partnership: This group of large business CEOs was formed in 2010 to give the commonwealth's largest employers a stronger voice. Led by Dan O'Connell, top Boston area CEOs, including Fidelity's Abby Johnson, Staples' Ron Sargent and State Street Corp's Jay Hooley, are among its 15 members.

The New England Council: This group helps connect businesses in New England with policy-makers in Washington. Led by Jim Brett, the group sponsors conversations with leading political figures, including presidential candidates. NEC's annual dinner in the fall draws over 1,400 attendees.

The Boston Club: A preeminent organization for women executives in the region, the Boston Club is dedicated to connecting women business leaders and professionals and helping advance the careers of women in the workplace. Led by executive director Constance Armstrong, the Boston Club offers an array of programming while also advocating for more women on corporate boards and the C-Suite.

Mass Technology Leadership Council: More commonly known at MassTLC, the group focuses on connecting and promoting Massachusetts' many tech clusters. Led by president and CEO Tom Hopcroft, MassTLC holds many events over the course of the year, including its Leadership Awards Gala.

Massachusetts Innovation and Technology Exchange (MITX): This group bills itself as "the premier Internet business and marketing association in New England," offering programming and networking events. Amy Quigley is the president.

Massachusetts Taxpayers Foundation: A leading watchdog on fiscal affairs involving state government, MTF weighs in on issues of taxation, regulation, and government reform of agencies. The group is led by president Eileen McAnneny.

Massachusetts Business Roundtable: This business group focuses on issues to make the Massachusetts economy more competitive, including STEM (science, technology, engineering, math) initiatives and promoting early childhood education. JD Chesloff leads the group.

Business groups are abundant and offer an opportunity to connect directly with decision-makers.

Alliance for Business Leadership: This group of business leaders, feeling that their voices weren't being heard in policy debates, formed a group to help push a more progressive business agenda. The group is led by executive director Jesse Mermell.

The Commonwealth Institute: This organization is focused on helping women executives and entrepreneurs achieve success. Its membership includes "CEOs, senior corporate executives, entrepreneurs, executive directors of nonprofits and solo professionals who are committed to building successful businesses, organizations and careers," according to its website.

The Massachusetts High Tech Council: Headed by longtime president Chris Anderson, the Mass. High Tech Council advocates for issues and policies to improve the Massachusetts business climate, especially in matters that relate to the state's high tech and defense clusters.

NAIOP Massachusetts is the region's premier commercial real estate business group. It's led by David Begelfer.

Retailers Association of Massachusetts: The voice of retail at the State House, the RAM often gets involved in public policy that most affect the retailing workforce, such as the minimum wage. Jon Hurst runs the group.

Massachusetts Biotechnology Council: As biotech has surged in Massachusetts, so has MassBio, its trade group. MassBio works on an array of public policy issues, organizes industry events, training and hosts a job board that has over 2,000 jobs as of late August 2015. Robert Coughlin is the group's CEO.

Massachusetts Society of CPAs: Led by Amy Pitter, former Commission of the state's Department of Revenue, the organization boasts 11,000 members. It provides advocacy, professional development and networking for its membership.

The Smaller Business Association of New England: Also know as SBANE, the association focuses on providing practical information to help business owners grow their companies, and also it is known for its New England Innovation Awards program. Bob Baker is the president of the organization.

The Ad Club: The region's premier trade group for advertising and marketing industry, the Ad Club is, according to its website, "Focused on networking, education, professional development, advocacy, and diversity." The Ad Club also organizes 30 events per year. It's run by longtime president Kathy Kiely.

Health care business groups include the Massachusetts Hospital Association and the Massachusetts Association of Health Plans. Together with the Massachusetts Medical Society, which is not technically a business group, they advocate for policies related to health care.

Other chambers of commerce: Greater Boston has many large regional chambers, including the South Shore Chamber (1,254 members as of May 1, 2015) led by President and CEO Peter Forman.

Pivotal eras and moments in Boston's economic history

From a colonial-era economy based largely on agriculture, small workshops and limited overseas trade, the Massachusetts economy has undergone major transformations over the centuries:

Whaling and clipper ship trade

Though it has always had a strong fishing-industry tradition, the Massachusetts economy thrived as a result of the early 1800s whaling trade that brought enormous wealth into the bustling ports of New Bedford, Nantucket and other coastal towns and cities. The same adventurous spirit applied to increasingly

Clipper ship Southern Cross leaving Boston Harbor, 1851, by Fitz Hugh Lane

aggressive Bay State merchants engaged in global sea trade, often using fast Clipper ships to haul goods.

Sidney & Neff, Detail from "Plan of the City of Lowell, Massachusetts," 1850.

Textiles and the Industrial Age

In Massachusetts, the Industrial Revolution arrived with the building of huge textile mills in Lowell and other riverfront communities in the 1830s and 1840s, ushering in a manufacturing era that extended through the American Civil War and to this day in Massachusetts. The Industrial Revolution not only shifted manufacturing from small workshops operated by craftsmen to huge factories employing thousands, it generated fortunes for local industrialists who later would transform the economy in other ways.

Ether experiments and the emergence of a medical-research industry

In 1846, physicians at the Massachusetts General Hospital conducted the first public demonstration of ether as a surgical anesthetic, a historic medical

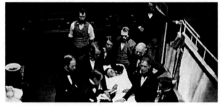

event that foreshadowed Boston's eventual rise as a medical-research mecca. In the early 1900s, Harvard opened a new medical school campus and helped establish the university's first teaching hospital — Peter Bent Brigham Hospital, now Brigham and Women's Hospital — in the then remote Fenway section of Boston. Known today as the Longwood Medical Area, the district is home to a number of world-renowned hospitals and medical-research institutes employing tens of thousands of workers.

Critical care and pain medicine traces its roots back to the October 16, 1846 public demonstration of medical ether.

The first tech era: Telephones, electricity and razor blades

In 1876, Alexander Graham Bell famously muttered the words, "Mr. Watson, come here" over a copper wire that transmitted actual sound. The telephone era was born. And it happened in Boston, where the world's first commercial telephone line was established a year later between Somerville and Boston. Other tech titans and innovations soon followed in the late 1800s, from the formation of General Electric (from the merger of Lynn-based Thomson-Houston Co. and Edison Electric Co.) to King Camp Gillette's use of highly skilled machinists to make new-fangled razor blades.

Alexander Graham Bell

Higher education: Engine of research and growth

Founded in 1636, Harvard University has long served as an academic powerhouse in Massachusetts and the United States. But in the 19th century, a number of other higher education institutions emerged that also later played critical roles in the development of the Massachusetts economy, including Boston University (founded in 1839) and Tufts University (1852), both of which today are major research institutions in Boston. The founding of the Massachusetts Institute of Technology in 1861 (in Boston's newly filled in Back Bay) ultimately had an even bigger impact, as MIT later developed into a world-class technology school whose faculty and students have created literally thousands of tech companies over the years. Today, Harvard and MIT often vie for the top spot in rankings of the world's best universities.

Rogers Building. MIT's first building; Back Bay, Boston, MA. 1889.

Mutual funds and venture capital

In 1924, the nation's first mutual fund was created in Boston by Massachusetts Investors Trust, later renamed Massachusetts Financial Services. At roughly the same time, State Street Research started its own mutual fund in Boston — and an "industry" was officially born. Today, Boston's mutual fund industry also includes Eaton Vance Corp. (founded in late 1924), Wellington Management (1928), Putnam Investments (1937) and Fidelity Investments (1946), today the world's largest actively managed mutual fund company.

In 1946, American Research and Development Corporation (ARD), a Massachusetts corporation, was founded by Georges Doriot, a Harvard Business School professor who considered by many as the "father of modern venture capital." The goal of the first ARD fund: To spread risk and encourage private sector investment in new tech products. Investors in ARD and other VC funds later based in Boston were often rich industrialists or their descendants looking for new ways to invest their money.

The second tech era: Radio tubes, defense and computers

Some point to the founding of Raytheon Co. in 1922 as the start of the modern technology era in Massachusetts. Known initially as American Appliance Co., Raytheon first made a go at producing refrigerators and then later vacuum tubes for radios. Buoyed by massive defense spending during World War II, Raytheon eventually became a defense-industry titan, developing radar products during the war and later the Patriot anti-missile system in the 1980s. Other local institutions boosted by WWII, Cold War and NASA spending included companies like Draper Laboratory and EG&G Inc.

But it wasn't just defense-related companies that helped develop the state's modern technology industry. In 1949, Edwin Land unveiled to an astonished world a new instant film-development camera produced by his company Polaroid Corp., itself founded in Cambridge in 1937. In the 1970s, computer companies — such as Digital Equipment, Wang Laboratories, Data General, Prime Computer and other firms, sometimes funded via young venture capital and private equity firms in the Boston area — began to take off. Many later floundered in the 1980s and 1990s, but they laid the groundwork for other large and startup tech companies to later thrive in the area.

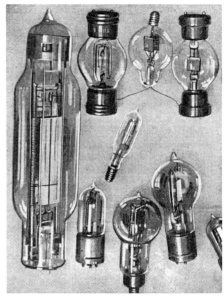

Early triode vacuum tubes belonging to American inventor Lee De Forest from 1920.

Biotechnology, pharmaceuticals and medical devices

A direct offshoot of the state's strong higher-education and health-care industries, the state's burgeoning biotech and pharmaceutical sectors can trace their beginnings to a number of specific sources. Among the early pioneers was the Whitehead Institute, founded to study molecular biology and genetics in Cambridge in 1982. The Whitehead's first director: David Baltimore, a Nobel laureate. Meanwhile, early corporate players included Biogen Inc. (founded in 1978) and Genzyme Corp. (1981), among others. They and other companies — including Boston Scientific, a major medical device firm — all contributed to an ecosystem that's made the Boston-Cambridge market the world leader today in cutting-edge research and development of medicines and other medical products.

The Whitehead Institute was one of the major centers for the Human Genome Project, which completed the sequencing of DNA and mapping of the genes of the human genome in 2003, an accomplishment that has ushered in a new era of targeted drug treatments.

What Bostonians make: A list of occupations and salaries over $100,000

(data from the Bureau of Labor Statistics, 2015 earnings)

Oral and Maxillofacial Surgeons	$268,670	Marketing Managers	$139,170
Anesthesiologists	$258,230	Economics Teachers, Postsecondary	$132,820
Obstetricians and Gynecologists	$249,510	Compensation and Benefits Managers	$132,720
Surgeons	$232,760	Financial Managers	$132,100
Internists, General	$230,440	General and Operations Managers	$131,810
Orthodontists	$225,620	Training and Development Managers	$131,600
Pediatricians, General	$222,480	Personal Financial Advisors	$130,200
Family and General Practitioners	$212,210	Advertising and Promotions Managers	$129,440
Chief Executives	$207,510	Political Science Teachers, Postsecondary	$126,950
Dentists, General	$179,390	Securities, Commodities, and Financial Services Sales Agents	$125,870
Dentists, All Other Specialists	$178,720	Health Specialties Teachers, Postsecondary	$122,540
Psychiatrists	$176,640	Computer and Information Research Scientists	$122,130
Natural Sciences Managers	$172,110	Managers, All Other	$120,690
Nurse Anesthetists	$167,160	Public Relations and Fundraising Managers	$120,660
Physicians and Surgeons, All Other	$161,730	Engineering Teachers, Postsecondary	$119,810
Lawyers	$152,990	Human Resources Managers	$119,690
Law Teachers, Postsecondary	$147,370	Legal Occupations	$118,830
Podiatrists	$147,230	Computer Network Architects	$118,110
Sales Managers	$146,380	Purchasing Managers	$116,250
Computer and Information Systems Managers	$145,550	Optometrists	$115,790
Administrative Law Judges, Adjudicators, and Hearing Officers	$140,660	Physics Teachers, Postsecondary	$115,300
Architectural and Engineering Managers	$140,210		
Business Teachers, Postsecondary	$139,500		

Sales Engineers	$114,320	Electronics Engineers, Except Computer	$107,660
Computer Hardware Engineers	$113,820	Construction Managers	$107,430
Pharmacists	$113,690	Chemistry Teachers, Postsecondary	$106,810
Atmospheric, Earth, Marine, and Space Sciences Teachers, Postsecondary	$113,630	Physical Scientists, All Other	$105,220
Industrial Production Managers	$113,430	Financial Analysts	$105,130
Software Developers, Systems Software	$113,410	Physician Assistants	$105,060
Nurse Practitioners	$112,860	Chemical Engineers	$104,980
Anthropology and Archeology Teachers, Postsecondary	$112,640	Psychology Teachers, Postsecondary	$102,600
Medical and Health Services Managers	$112,050	Management Analysts	$101,950
Veterinarians	$112,040	Sales Representatives, Wholesale and Manufacturing, Technical and Scientific Products	$101,420
Actuaries	$111,780		
Real Estate Brokers	$111,530	Administrative Services Managers	$101,400
Aerospace Engineers	$110,800	Financial Examiners	$101,290
Mathematicians	$110,120	Education Administrators, Elementary and Secondary School	$101,280
Engineers, All Other	$109,980		
Software Developers, Applications	$109,430	Funeral Service Managers	$101,130
Nurse Midwives	$108,710	Area, Ethnic, and Cultural Studies Teachers, Postsecondary	$100,680
Art Directors	$108,590		
Electrical Engineers	$107,820	Biological Science Teachers, Postsecondary	$100,460

Index of companies and people